Andrew Johnson

ANDREW JOHNSON,

PRESIDENT OF THE UNITED STATES;

HIS LIFE AND SPEECHES.

BY

LILLIAN FOSTER,

AUTHOR OF "WAYSIDE GLIMPSES NORTH AND SOUTH," &C.

NEW YORK:

RICHARDSON & CO.,

540 BROADWAY.

1866.

PREFACE.

The future of our country depends so much upon the distinguished and remarkable individual who now occupies the Presidential Chair, that a portrait of his life and character, adapted to general use, cannot fail to receive a favorable reception from the entire community. Such a biographical sketch, written by a countrywoman of the Chief Magistrate, may also be supposed to interest, in a particular manner, that sex who have suffered so fearfully during the late terrible war, and who now rejoice with all their hearts at the prospects of Peace, Union, and Prosperity which the noble and patriotic conduct of the President is rapidly restoring to every section of the great Republic.

A true-hearted woman naturally admires and appreciates great and heroic excellence. Her tribute of esteem and gratitude for brave and magnanimous actions is shadowed by no jealousy and colored by no party opinions.

With such feelings, I present to my countrymen and especially to my countrywomen, this brief narration of the life and public services of His Excellency President Andrew Johnson, believing him to be a statesman whose whole intellect is devoted to the greatest good of the entire United States, and whose admirable policy of restoration commends itself to the warmest approbation and the most zealous support of the best and wisest portion of the American people.

CONTENTS.

CHAPTER VI.

CHAPTER VII.

CHAPTER VIII.

CHAPTER IX.

CHAPTER X.

CHAPTER XI.

CHAPTER XII.

CHAPTER XIII.

CHAPTER XIV.

CHAPTER XV.

CHAPTER XVI.

CHAPTER XVII.

CHAPTER XVIII.

CHAPTER XIX.

BIOGRAPHICAL INTRODUCTION.

At the beginning of the present century there resided in Raleigh, the capital of North Carolina, a couple who were pecuniarily in circumstances which excluded them from a social position with their more wealthy and aristocratic neighbors; yet within that humble abode the young wife gave birth to a son, who was destined to achieve the highest position by his commanding intellect and exalted moral worth.

Andrew Johnson was born on the 29th day of December, 1808. While still in his fifth year, his father lost his life by injuries received through magnanimous and successful efforts to save Col. Thomas Henderson, editor of the Raleigh Gazette, from drowning,—leaving his wife and young son dependent upon their own efforts for future support. The calamitous event of his father's death prevented the son from receiving even an ordinary education. The admirable system of common or free schools, which are now enjoyed by the poor children of the whole country, is a blessing which at that time had not been experienced by North Carolina, and consequently young Johnson was never enabled to receive an hour's instruction in a schoolroom. At the early age of ten years he was apprenticed to a tailor, in his native town, until he was seventeen. Applying himself steadily to his trade for his own and mother's support, he was left without any resource but in his own exertions, and he thus began life struggling with the rough business world, but with a heart that stoutly battled poverty and misfortune, and that soon won him the confidence and respect of even the most wealthy and respectable portion of the community in which he resided.

In the company of his associates he felt the great want of the learning which fortune denied him, and at once resolved to remedy the deficiency by all the means which energy and time could command. A gentleman residing in town made frequent visits to the tailor's shop, who enlightened the minds and lightened the hours of toil by reading to the workmen. The book selected (a collection of speeches by British statesmen) so interested and aroused the ambition of young Johnson, that his mind was indoctrinated with principles and ideas which in after-years were developed in the halls of Congress. He devoted the hours after his day's work was done to learning the alphabet, which he soon mastered; and then he asked the loan of the book, that he might learn to spell. The owner, instead of loaning, gave him the work, and also instructed him in the formation of words. Through perseverance and patience, aided by a strong resolution to surmount all obstacles, success crowned his efforts; and to his great delight he found himself able to read the speeches to which he had only a short time before been an interested listener.

The term of his apprenticeship having expired in 1824, he went to Laurens Courthouse, S. C., where he worked as a journeyman until May, 1826, when he returned to Raleigh. There he remained until September of that year, when, in company with his mother, he removed to Greenville, a small town in Eastern Tennessee, at which place he obtained work. Not many months elapsed after his settlement in Greenville before he married a young woman, whose mental attainments and devoted affection exerted a very beneficial influence on his future life. Sympathizing in the desires of her husband to acquire an education, and in his ambition to rise to distinction, scarcely had the marriage ceremony been performed before this estimable woman commenced instructing, by her conversation, and reading to him when employed on his work-bench, thus lightening his labor by her constant oral instruction. At night, when the day's work was done, the instructions were continued by lessons in writing and arithmetic. Stimulated by ambition, by unceasing perseverance and an indomitable will the poor tailor boy soon became proficient in reading, writing, and arithmetic, and was not long in ripening into a thorough English scholar. While this romantic part of their history was in progress, Mr. Johnson, thinking to better his condition by removing West, left Greenville; but after an absence of some months he returned to his former home, where he permanently settled. The broad and enlightened views of the more liberal British statesmen, engrafted on his mind by the readings in the old workshop, and by his future studies of the principles of republican government—a government of the people, by the people, and for the people—formed the basis of that system of political philosophy which has rendered Mr. Johnson conspicuous among the most enlightened statesmen of his country.

From the very commencement of Mr. Johnson's career he devoted himself to the interest and welfare of the toiling and laboring masses. From their ranks he had sprung, and upon them in reality rest the hopes and glory of our country. He soon became known as the most able advocate of the working men in Greenville. To advance the true interest of the masses of the people, he used his influence to assert their right to representation in the town councils. In 1828 the young tailor was triumphantly elected alderman in Greenville, which position he held until

1830, when he was elected mayor, and served in that capacity for three succeeding years, at the same time holding the position of trustee of Rhea Academy, to which he had been appointed by the County Court. In 1834 he bore a conspicuous part in the adoption of the new Constitution of Tennessee, and established his reputation as one of the foremost men of his State.

In 1835 he was elected a member of the House of Representatives of the State, for the counties of Green and Washington. He distinguished himself in that body more particularly by his earnest opposition to a grand scheme of internal improvement, which he contended would prove a failure ; and also denounced it as a base fraud, tending to impoverish the State treasury and cripple the resources of the commonwealth. This opposition rendered him unpopular at the time, and prevented his re-election in 1837. The passage of the bill he had opposed proved, as he had predicted, a useless burden to the people ; and in 1839 he was again returned to the Legislature.

In 1840, in the contest between General Harrison and Martin Van Buren, Mr. Johnson was one of the Presidential Electors on the Democratic ticket, and canvassed the State for Mr. Van Buren,—not unfrequently meeting upon the stump some of the most able orators of the opposition, with whom he not only competed successfully, but excelled the ablest of them in the force and power of his reasoning. In 1841 he was sent to the State Senate from Green and Hawkins counties, and, while in that body, introduced some excellent and judicious projects for internal improvements in Eastern Tennessee. In the Senate, as in the lower branch of the Legislature, he proved himself a foremost member ; ever advocating all that he believed to be right, and fearlessly denouncing that which he deemed wrong.

The people, feeling entire confidence in his abilities and appreciating his services, resolved to extend his sphere of usefulness ; and in 1843 he was nominated for Congress in the First District of Tennessee, embracing seven counties. His opponent, Colonel John A. Asken, a United States Bank Democrat, a gentleman of prominence and ability, he handsomely defeated, and in December of the same year took his seat in the House of Representatives at Washington, retaining the position, by successive elections, until 1853.

His State was redistricted previous to 1853, and that portion in which Mr. Johnson resided was so districted as to place him in a district having a large Whig majority ; and thus he lost his seat in Congress. Gustavus A. Henry, who was at that time Whig candidate for governor, used his influence to effect this party trick, and Mr. Johnson, in return, determined to defeat the man who had resorted to such a measure to shut him out of Congress. After an exciting canvass,

Mr. Johnson was chosen governor. In 1855 he was re-elected, defeating one of the ablest Whigs in the State, Meredith P. Gentry. The duties of his administration were performed without regard to party, and it was confessed that he was one of the ablest and most impartial governors ever elected in that State.

In the year 1857, Mr. Johnson was elected by the Legislature of Tennessee United States senator for the full term of six years; and he brought to this high position the same indomitable energy, talent, and devotion to the people's welfare which had distinguished his whole public life. He was regarded as one of the ablest members of the Senate, and faithfully stood by the interest of his State until it joined the Confederacy, when he stood by the old Union, and was appointed Military Governor of Tennessee in 1862.

Mr. Johnson was a representative of *the people.* Born of the people, and at an early age thrown upon his own resources, he grew up amongst the people, becoming familiar with their lives, their wrongs, their wants, and their rights. Proud that for the knowledge he possessed he was indebted solely to his own exertions, he stood in the halls of Congress—Andrew Johnson, Tailor and Statesman, the equal of any member of either House. Modestly appreciating the dignity of his position, he never permitted a scoff at his calling, or an indignity at the laboring classes, to pass unrebuked. He, on one occasion, said:

"Sir, I do not forget that I am a mechanic. I am proud to own it. Neither do I forget that Adam was a tailor, and sewed fig-leaves, or that our Saviour was the son of a carpenter."

He had great aversion to aristocracy, and perhaps was not without prejudices against gentlemen reared in affluence and idleness, arrogating to themselves the claim to all respectability in the world. On one occasion Jefferson Davis superciliously asked: "What do you mean by the laboring classes?" Andrew Johnson replied: "Those who earn their bread by the sweat of their face, and not by fatiguing their ingenuity."

He was a true Democrat, and a firm believer in the sovereignty of the people: respecting statesmen and hating politicians—holding that legislation was for the many, and not for the benefit of any party. He was consistently in favor of curtailment in governmental expenses, and participated in nearly every debate upon appropriation bills. He introduced resolutions to reduce the salaries of members of Congress, and all officers of the government, civil, military, and naval. He opposed all unnecessary appropriations in Congress, from his dislike to "speculations and jobs."

He was the faithful friend of the poor and of the laboring classes, and ever appeared in Congress as their champion. He introduced the subject of homesteads into the House of Representatives, and advocated the cause with success in that branch. He also brought up the subject in the Senate, and debated it at great length; but the bill, as passed, was vetoed by Mr. Buchanan. He proposed an amendment to the tariff bill, with a view of taxing capital instead of labor. He also opposed the tariff on tea and sugar.

He advocated the bill to refund the fine imposed upon Andrew Jackson by Judge Hall at New Orleans (House of Representatives, Jan. 8, 1844); was in favor of the annexation of Texas (H. R., January 21, 1845); discussed the Oregon question, asserting our right to 54° 40′, but sustained the administration in the final settlement of the question (H. R., January 31, 1846); addressed the House on the Mexican question, in support of the administration, December 15, 1846, January 5, 1847, and August 2, 1847; opposed the bill establishing the courts of claims (H. R., January 6, 1849); made an earnest plea for the admission of California, and the protection of slavery (H. R., June 5, 1850); debated the Mexican indemnity bill (H. R., January 21, 28, 1852); also the bill for right of way on rail and plank roads (H. R., July 20, 1852); made a speech on frauds in the Treasury Department (H. R., January 13, 1853); and another on coinage (H. R., February 2, 1853).

While in the Senate, in addition to the measures referred to more at length in this sketch, he opposed the increase of the regular army at the time of the Mormon difficulties (Senate, February 17, 1857); had an earnest debate with Honorable John Bell, his colleague, on the Tennessee resolutions inviting Bell to resign (Senate, February 23, 24, 1857); participated in the debate on the admission of Minnesota (Senate, April 6, 1858); opposed the Pacific Railroad bill, and repudiated the idea that it could be imposed upon him as a Democratic measure (Senate, January 25, 1859); advocated retrenchment (Senate, January 4 and February 12, 1859); and warmly defended Tennessee (Senate, March 26, 1860).

A native of a slave State, and himself the owner of slaves, "acquired by the toil of his own hands," he accepted slavery as it existed. Strong in the belief that the agitation of the subject would eventually lead to the abolition of slavery, and the dissolution of the Union would naturally follow, he opposed its introduction into the debates of Congress, and was one of those who disbelieved the right to petition upon the subject, giving his reasons in a speech delivered January 31st, 1844:

"My position is, that Congress has no power to interfere with the subject of slavery; that it is an institution local in its character and peculiar to the States where it exists, and no other power has the right to control it."*

* Speech in the House of Representatives, June 5th, 1860.

He continued true to this belief, and was consistent in his course to the very last, and in the stormy scenes in the Senate, in December, 1860, we find him demanding new guaranties for the perpetuity of slavery.

But it needed the severe trial of the crisis of 1860 and 1861 to develop the strong points in his character, and to discover his sincere love for and undeviating honesty to the Union. In those dark days, when each man was suspicious of his neighbor, the country demanded men of strength—with comprehension to grasp the great question of the day—to discern its bearings upon the future; men, "bold to take up, firm to sustain," the glorious flag of a commonwealth of States. Few who passed through and were tried by the fierce ordeal of those terrible hours came forth a wiser statesman and more honest patriot than Andrew Johnson.

An ardent admirer of Andrew Jackson, the memorable words of that invincible patriot—"The Union, it must and shall be preserved"—were deeply imprinted on his heart. In a speech, delivered in the House of Representatives, December 19th, 1846, in support of the policy of Mr. Polk's administration in carrying the war into Mexico, he had said:

"I am in favor of supporting the administration in this act, because I believe it to be right. But, sir, I care not whether right or wrong, *I am for my country always.*"

In December, 1859, he had denounced the John Brown raid on Harper's Ferry, and said he believed it to be the legitimate fruit of abolition teachings. He wished for the punishment of its leaders under the Constitution, for a hostile entrance into a sovereign State. Under the same Constitution, he remained firm in 1860, after the election of Abraham Lincoln to the presidency, and feared none of the visions which so disturbed the imagination of a majority of the Southern senators and representatives. In view of the increasing excitement at the South, he thought the North should be willing to give some new constitutional guaranties for the protection of slavery, and introduced resolutions to that effect, December 13th, 1860, which were referred to the select committee of thirteen. Five days later, in a powerful speech, he appealed to the Southern senators to remain in the Union, and "fight for their constitutional rights on the battlements of the Constitution." He did not mean to be driven out of the Union, and if anybody must go out, it must be those who have violated the instrument that binds us together by passing personal liberty bills and opposing the execution of the fugitive slave law.

At the first session of the Thirty-seventh Congress, in July and August, 1861, he submitted the credentials of the senators from West Virginia, with appropriate remarks. On the 26th of July, 1861, he introduced a resolution defining the objects of the war, as follows :

"*Resolved.* That the present deplorable civil war has been forced upon the country by the disunionists of the Southern States, now in revolt against the Constitutional Government, and in arms around the capital; that in this national emergency, Congress, banishing all feeling of mere passion or resentment, will recollect only its duty to the whole country; that this war is not prosecuted upon our part in any spirit of oppression, nor for any purpose of conquest or subjugation, nor for the purpose of authorizing or interfering with the rights or established institutions of those States, but to defend and maintain the supremacy of the Constitution and all laws made in pursuance thereof; and to preserve the Union, with all the dignity, equality, and rights of the several States, unimpaired; that as soon as these objects are accomplished, the war ought to cease."

This was passed after a long debate, by a vote of thirty to five.

On the 31st of January, 1862, he made a determined speech on the conduct of Senator Bright, and voted for expelling the man who, four years before, had administered to him the senatorial oath.

From the outset of the rebellion, the course of Mr. Johnson did not please the secessionists of Tennessee or of the whole South. Mob law prevailed, and ruffians, full of malice, and with the ferocity of brutes, had inaugurated a reign of terror, and citizens who remained loyal to the Union were subjected to every possible indignity and persecution. He left Washington in April, 1861, at the close of the session of Congress, and on the 21st of that month he suffered personal peril at Lynchburg, Virginia, and at various places along his route. A price was set upon his head, and personal violence threatened if he remained in Tennessee. Such seeming indignities were the more honorable to him, inasmuch as they arose from his noble devotion to principle, when strong men failed and yielded to what they feebly claimed to be the real "sentiment" of their State in reference to secession.

On the 19th of June, 1861, while on his way to Washington to attend the special session of Congress, he was the recipient of a warm public welcome from the loyal people of Cincinnati. On that occasion he delivered an able address, defining his position, from which we will give a short extract, not having space for the entire speech :

" So far as I am concerned, I am willing to say in this connection, that I am proud to stand here among you as one of the humble upholders and supporters of the stars and stripes that have been borne by Washington through a seven years' revolution—a bold and manly struggle for our independence, and separation from the mother country. That is my flag—that flag was borne by Washington in triumph. Under it I want to live, and under no other. It is that flag that has been borne in triumph by the revolutionary fathers over every battle-field, when our brave men, after toil and danger, laid down and slept on the cold ground, with no covering but the inclement sky, and arose in the morning and renewed their march over the frozen ground, as the blood trickled from their feet—all to protect that banner and bear it aloft triumphantly."

While in Washington, he urged upon the President and Secretary of War the importance and the justice of aiding and protecting the Unionists of East Tennessee, that Switzerland of America. Meanwhile, in the eastern portion of that State, Confederates confiscated Mr. Johnson's slaves; went to his home, drove his sick wife, with her child, into the street; and turned their house, built by his own hands, into a hospital and barracks.

In February, 1862, General Grant entered Tennessee, and won the great victories of Fort Henry and Fort Donelson. The subsequent advance of General Buell's forces compelled the withdrawal of the main body of the insurgents from Western and Middle Tennessee, and Nashville was rendered indefensible. The Confederate government of the State was therefore removed to Memphis. The larger portion of the State having been thus recovered, and in the occupation of the Federal forces, President Lincoln appointed Andrew Johnson military governor, with the rank of brigadier-general of volunteers. On the 5th of March, 1862, the Senate confirmed the appointment, and Governor Johnson left his seat in that body to enter upon the duties of his new position.

We cannot conceive of a more fitting appointment than this. He had borne many personal indignities ; his family had been mercilessly persecuted : but threats could not intimidate him. He promised that the rights of the people should be respected, and their wrongs redressed ; that the loyal should be honored, and the erring and misguided should be welcomed on their return ; intelligent and conscious treason should be punished—boldly proclaiming that traitors should be hung. Dauntless but just, determined but compassionate, he was the man of all men to rule with firmness in such times. The man who uttered words like these in a border State, amidst anarchy and a fierce civil war, and set to work in right earnest to verify his prediction, is assuredly no common man. Mr. Johnson, with the inspiration of a true man of genius, believed in his own powers, and felt they must ultimately prevail. He reached Nashville on the 12th of March, in company with Horace Maynard, Emerson Etheridge, and others who had been political exiles. He was enthusiastically received by the long suffering Unionists ; and in response to a serenade, addressed the assemblage, which address he afterwards published as "An appeal to the people of Tennessee." In this address he sketched the history of the secession movement, and showed how the government of the Commonwealth had been wrecked for the time by its leaders. He said that the Government of the United States could do no less than guarantee Tennessee a republican form of government, and that his work was to accomplish that purpose. Later in March, Governor Johnson ordered the mayor and city council of Nashville to take the oath of allegiance. Upon their refusing so to do, their places were proclaimed vacant, and other officials were appointed. It was soon understood that spoken or written disunionism would subject the transgressors to similar justice; which was carried out by incarcerating Turner S. Foster, a well-known secessionist, who had been recently chosen judge of the Circuit Court of Nashville. The clergymen of the city, who, with the exception of the Catholic, not only entertained disunion sentiments, but boldly preached them from their pulpits, were requested by the governor to take the oath of allegiance. They obeyed the summons so far as to appear before Governor Johnson, who, perfectly composed, entered the room, shaking hands familiarly with two or three of them, and said: "Well, gentlemen, what is your desire?" They requested a few days to consider the subject of signing the paper. The governor granted them a week, and said to them: "It seems to me that there should be but little hesitation among you, gentlemen, about the matter. All that is required of you is to sign the oath of allegiance.

If you are loyal citizens you can have no reason to refuse to do so. If you are disloyal, and working to obstruct the operations of the Government, it is my duty, as the representative of that Government, to see that you are placed in a position so that the least possible harm can result from your proceedings. You certainly cannot reasonably refuse to renew your allegiance to the Government that is now protecting you and your families and property."

At the expiration of a week the clergymen signified to Governor Johnson their determination not to take the oath, and were sent to the penitentiary, prior to their removal to General Halleck's quarters, to be exchanged for Union prisoners.

In September, General Buell evacuated all North Alabama and Southern Tennessee. Governor Johnson deplored the wholesale desertion of the country, and did not concur with General Buell as to its propriety. On the 5th the enemy recaptured Murfreesboro'. On the 6th Nashville was thrown into a state of great excitement, in consequence of a current report that General Buell had determined upon the evacuation of the city. When the rumor reached Governor Johnson, he earnestly protested against such a course, asserting that the city should be defended to the last extremity, and then destroyed, to prevent its falling into the hands of the enemy. He was so disgusted with General Buell's movements, that he addressed a letter to President Lincoln on the subject, and recommended his removal. General Thomas, who was placed in command of the city, heartily sustained Governor Johnson's determination, and the city was strongly fortified. Afterwards General Negley was assigned to the command.

These months proved a dark and perilous time for the citizens of Nashville and the safety of the provisional government. The State was infested with guerrillas, and the Confederate forces, under Kirby Smith and others, moved northward through Tennessee to invade Kentucky. At times Nashville was wholly isolated—its communications cut off in every direction; provisions became scarce, prices enormously high, and much suffering prevailed. Through all these trying times Governor Johnson remained hopeful and self-reliant, inspiring confidence in all around him, and reviving courage by his calmness and determination. Many of the inhabitants of Nashville, whose fathers, husbands, brothers, and sons were in arms against the Government, left their families to be cared for by the authorities. To remedy this, the Governor addressed the following circular to such of the avowed secessionists of the city as were pecuniarily able to respond:

STATE OF TENNESSEE, EXECUTIVE DEPARTMENT,
NASHVILLE, August 18, 1862.

SIR—There are many wives and helpless children in the city of Nashville and county of Davidson, who have been reduced to poverty and wretchedness in consequence of their husbands and fathers having been forced into the armies of this unholy and nefarious rebellion. Their necessities have become so manifest, and their demands for the necessaries of life so urgent, that the laws of justice and humanity would be violated unless something was done to relieve their suffering and destitute condition.

You are therefore requested to contribute the sum of —— dollars, which you will pay over within the next five days to James Whitworth, Esq., Judge of the County Court, to be by him distributed among these destitute families in such manner as may be prescribed.

Respectfully, etc.,
ANDREW JOHNSON,
Military Governor.

Attest:
EDWARD H. EAST, Secretary of State.

After several attacks upon the city, which were gallantly repulsed by General Negley, the Confederates were forced to retire, as General Rosecrans, who had relieved General Buell, was advancing from the direction of Bowling Green. In November the forces under command of the latter general entered the city, and found its defenders on half-rations, but still full of courage and determination. In October, Governor Johnson's family rejoined him, after incurring and escaping numerous perils while on their journey from Bristol, in the northeastern part of the State.

On the 13th of December, Governor Johnson

issued an order nearly identical with his circular of August 18th, assessing the property of the enemies of the Government to the amount of sixty thousand dollars, for the support of the poor, the widows, and the orphans, made so by the war.

After the retreat of General Bragg from Murfreesboro', in July, 1863, West and Middle Tennessee were entirely under Federal control. Burnside then advanced into East Tennessee and drove the insurgents out. A convention was held at Nashville, in September, to consider the restoration of Tennessee to the Union. Governor Johnson thus expressed his views on that question: "Tennessee is not out of the Union—never has been, and never will be out. The bonds of the Constitution and the Federal power will always prevent that. This Government is perpetual: provision is made for reforming the Government and amending the Constitution, and admitting States into the Union; not for letting them out of it." He told the people, whenever they desired, in good faith, to restore civil authority, they could do so, and a proclamation for an election would be issued as speedily as it should become practicable to hold one.

The provisional government created by the President continued throughout the year, and on the 26th of January, 1864, Governor Johnson issued his proclamation for a State election. Up to this time about twenty-five thousand Union citizens of Tennessee entered the army, and several colored regiments were organized.

The country will remember the daring impromptu speech in the United States Senate, which Senator, now President Johnson, delivered in immediate reply to Jefferson Davis, when the latter took his farewell, and sought to demonstrate the inability of our Government to execute its properly constituted will upon the people of the States. Senator Johnson then stood alone. The disunionists had resolved to adopt every conceivable method known to them for the purpose of bending the inflexibility of his resolution to stand by the Union; but when they found that they had wholly failed, they treated him with open scorn and contempt. Great is the change since that scene in the Senate Chamber, when Davis was boldly confronted, answered, and denounced by the Tennessee senator;—the former incarcerated within the walls of a prison, awaiting his trial for treason, while Johnson is to-day the President of the United States. It is one of those lessons in the history of nations which are too marked to be forgotten.

Two notable incidents in the history of Andrew Johnson, as military governor of Tennessee, illustrative of indomitable will and dauntless courage, we think worthy of record.

A placard was posted in Nashville one morning, announcing that Andy Johnson was to be shot "on sight." Friends of the governor assembled at his house to escort him to the State House. "No," said he, "gentlemen, if I am to be shot at, I want no man to be in the way of the bullet." He walked alone, and with his usual deliberation, through the streets to his official apartments on Capitol Hill. Another similar story is related:

He was announced to speak on the exciting questions of the day, and loud threats were uttered that, if he dared to appear, he should not leave the hall alive. At the appointed hour he ascended the platform, and advancing to the desk laid his pistol upon it. He then addressed the audience, it is said, in the following language: "Fellow-citizens, it is proper, when freemen assemble for the discussion of important public interests, that every thing should be done decently and in order. I have been informed that part of the business to be transacted on the present occasion is the assassination of the individual who now has the honor of addressing you. I beg respectfully to propose this be the first business in order. Therefore, if any man has come here to-night for the purpose indicated, I do not say to him, let him speak, but let him shoot." Here he paused, with his right hand on his pistol, and the other holding open his coat, while he blandly surveyed the assembly. After a pause of half a minute, he resumed: "Gentlemen, it appears that I have been misinformed. I will now proceed to address you on the subject that has called us together," which he did with all his accustomed boldness and vivacity, not sparing his adversaries, but giving them plenty of pure Tennessee.

A man who sets out in a political career without high birth, fortune, political influence, or commercial interest at his back, determined not to be intimidated, discouraged, or run down by any party, or by all factions in Congress, and triumphs solely by his intellectual power over all impediments, must have the true elements of greatness in his composition. If such a man lends the powers that are in him for objects that are only noble, generous, grand, and good, he will be faithful to himself, and likely to be eminently useful to his country. Such is the character and such the position of President Johnson. Few men in the world have risen to greater fame from the ranks of poverty and misfortune; and none have ever worn their honors with a more becoming dignity, or with greater love for the sacred principles of free government.

SERVICES AND SPEECHES.

CHAPTER I.

THE CONSTITUTIONALITY AND RIGHTFULNESS OF SECESSION.

THE purely sectional issue upon which Abraham Lincoln, in November, 1860, was elected President of the United States, though in accordance with the forms of the Constitution, yet seemed to a large majority of the people so hostile to its spirit, and so threatening in its effect upon the peace of the country, that "it produced an excitement in the nation, and especially at the South, which foreboded all that was fearful and terrible in the prospect of the future." To allay this excitement so far as possible, and prevent the withdrawal of the aggrieved States from the Federal Union, all true patriots labored with heart and soul, during the anxious and critical period which intervened between the election of Mr. Lincoln and his inauguration. Among these patriots and statesmen, no one strove with a more earnest and indefatigable zeal to avert the dissolution of the Union and the horrors of civil war than Andrew Johnson. He supported the famous Crittenden compromise, in the hope that its adoption might promote harmony of feeling and quiet the rage of the dark and fearful storm. Born in a slave State, a representative, a governor, and senator from a slave State, his love for his section was only surpassed by his attachment to his country. Soaring above all narrow and local prejudices, he could truly feel and express the poet's inspiring sentiment:

> Who would sever freedom's shrine?
> Who would draw the invidious line?
> Though by birth one spot be mine,
> Dear is all the rest.
> Dear to me the South's fair land,
> Dear the central mountain band,
> Dear New England's rocky strand,
> Dear the prairied West.

But though national in every pulsation of his moral being, as became a disciple of the immortal Jackson, no one defended with more outspoken boldness the rights of his section, or denounced with more bitter indignation the wicked and treasonable designs of Northern abolitionism. He repeatedly deprecated the introduction of the slavery question into the congressional debates, insisting that its consideration belonged alone to the States where it existed, and refused even the admission of petitions in relation to the initiating subject. In December, 1859, he declared the murderous John Brown raid upon Harper's Ferry to be the natural consequence of abolition doctrines, and permitted no opportunity to escape of lashing and denouncing the advocates of a "higher law" than that of the Constitution. He had, however, the sagacity to see that the best protection for Southern rights and Southern property was beneath the folds of the Federal flag; that the surest way to punish the Northern agitators and nullifiers for their "personal-liberty bills" and similar insolent encroachments, was to fight them *inside of the Union*, and never to yield a single inch of the joint and common revolutionary inheritance. He entreated his fellow-senators of the South to remain in their places, assuring them that, if they thus remained firm and unshaken, Mr. Lincoln could not even organize his administration unless by their permission; and much less could he or his party do any direct injury to the Southern interests. With prophetic vision, he told them that secession would be the death of negro slavery, that in the blast of a sectional conflict it would be swept away with the besom of destruction. Alas! if his counsels and warnings had been heeded, how much of blood and sorrow, how much of woe and desolation, would have been spared from the record of these last sad years!

These opinions of Mr. Johnson are given at length, and with signal ability, in a speech delivered in the Senate, 18th and 19th of December, 1860, the question being the joint resolution introduced by him the 13th of the same month, proposing certain constitutional amendments. One of these amendments proposed to change the mode of electing the President and Vice-President of the United States from the electoral college to a vote more directly by the suffrages of the people. We cannot better please and instruct our readers than by placing before them some extracts from this admirable and remarkable speech. He said :

"It is not my purpose, sir, to discuss these propositions to amend the Constitution in detail to-day, and I shall say but little more in reference to them, and to their practical operation ; but as we are now, as it were, involved in revolution (for there is a revolution, in fact, upon the country), I think it behooves every man, and especially every one occupying a public place, to indicate, in some manner, his opinions and sentiments in reference to the questions that agitate and distract the public mind. I shall be frank on this occasion in giving my views and taking my position, as I have always been upon questions that involve the public interest. I believe it is the imperative duty of Congress to make some effort to save the country from impending dissolution ; and he that is unwilling to make an effort to preserve the Union, or, in other words, to preserve the Constitution, and the Union as an incident resulting from the preservation of the Constitution, is unworthy of public confidence, and the respect and gratitude of the American people.

"In most that I shall say on this occasion, I shall not differ very essentially from my Southern friends. The difference will consist in the mode and manner by which this great end is to be accomplished. Some of our Southern friends think that secession is the mode by which these ends can be accomplished; that if the Union cannot be preserved in its spirit, by secession they will get those rights secured and perpetuated that they have failed to obtain within the Union.

"I am opposed to secession. I believe it is no remedy for the evils complained of. Instead of acting with that division of my Southern friends who take ground for secession, I shall take other grounds while I try to accomplish the same end. I think that this battle ought to be fought, not outside but inside of the Union, and upon the battlements of the Constitution itself. I am unwilling voluntarily to walk out of the Union, which has been the result of a Constitution made by the patriots of the Revolution. They formed the Constitution; and this Union that is so much spoken of, and which all of us are so desirous to preserve, grows out of the Constitution; and I repeat, I am not willing to walk out of a Union growing out of the Constitution that was formed by the patriots and soldiers of the Revolution. So far as I am concerned, and I believe I may speak with some degree of confidence for the people of my State, we intend to fight that battle inside and not outside of the Union; and if anybody must go out of the Union, it must be those who violate it. We do not intend to go out. It is our Constitution; it is our Union, growing out of the Constitution; and we do not intend to be driven from it, or out of the Union. Those who have violated the Constitution, either in the passage of what are denominated personal-liberty bills, or by their refusal to execute the fugitive-slave law, they, having violated the instrument that binds us together, must go out, and not we. If we violate the Constitution by going out ourselves, I do not think we can go before the country with the same force of opinion that we shall if we stand inside of the Constitution, demanding a compliance with its provisions and its guaranties, or, if need be, as I think it is, demanding additional securities. We should make that demand inside of the Constitution, and in the manner and mode pointed out by the instrument itself. Then we keep ourselves in the right; we put our adversary in the wrong; and though it may take a little longer, we take the right means to accomplish an end that is right in itself.

"I know that sometimes we talk about compromises. I am not a compromiser nor a conservative, in the usual acceptation of those terms. I have been generally considered radical, and I do not come forward to-day, in any thing that I shall say or propose, asking for any thing to be done upon the principle of compromise. If we ask for any thing, it should be for that which is right and reasonable in itself. If it be right, those of whom we ask it, upon the great principle of right, are bound to grant it. Compromise! I know, in the common acceptation of the term, it is to agree upon certain propositions, in which some things are conceded on one side, and others conceded on the other. I shall go for enactments by Congress, or for amendments to the Constitution, upon the principle that they are right, and upon no other ground. I am not for compromising right with wrong. If we have no right, we ought not to demand it. If we are in the wrong, they should not grant us what we ask. I approach this momentous subject on the great principles of right, asking for nothing and demanding nothing but what is right in itself, and what every right-minded man, and a right-minded community, and a right-minded people, who wish for the preservation of this Government, will be disposed to grant.

* * * * *

"Sir, if the doctrine of secession is to be carried out upon the mere whim of a State, this Government is at an end. I am as much opposed to a strong, or what may be called by some a consolidated Government, as it is possible for a man to be; but while I am greatly opposed to that, I want a Government strong enough to preserve its own existence; that will not fall to pieces by its own weight, or whenever a little dissatisfaction takes place in one of its members. If the States have a right to secede at will and pleasure, for real or imaginary evils or oppressions, I repeat again, this Government is at an end; it is not stronger than a rope of sand; its own weight will crumble it to pieces, and it cannot exist. Notwithstanding this doctrine may suit some who are engaged in this perilous and impending crisis that is now upon us, duty to my country, duty to my State, and duty to my kind, require me to avow a doctrine that I believe will result in the preservation of th Government, and to repudiate one that I believe wi result in its overthrow, and the consequent disaster to the people of the United States.

"If a State can secede at will and pleasure, and thi doctrine is maintained, why, I ask, on the other hand as argued by Mr. Madison in one of his letters, can not a majority of the States combine and reject State out of the Confederacy? Have a majority o these States, under the compact that they have mad with each other, the right to combine and reject an one of the States from the Confederacy? They hav no such right; the compact is reciprocal. It wa ratified without reservation or condition, and it wa ratified '*in toto* and forever;' such is the language o James Madison; and there is but one way to get ou of it without the consent of the parties, and that i by revolution.

* * * * *

"I know that the term, to 'coerce a State,' is used in an *ad captandum* manner. It is a sovereignty that is to be crushed! How is a State in the Union? What is her connection with it? All the connection she has with the other States is that which is agreed upon in the compact between the States. I do not know whether you may consider it in the Union or out of the Union, or whether you simply consider it a connection or a disconnection with the other States; but to the extent that a State nullifies or sets aside any law or any provision of the Constitution, to that extent it has dissolved its connection, and no more. I think the States that have passed their personal-liberty bills, in violation of the Constitution of the

United States, coming in contact with the fugitive-slave law, to that extent have dissolved their connection, and to that extent it is revolution. But because some of the free States have passed laws violative of the Constitution; because they have, to some extent, dissolved their connection with this Government, does that justify us of the South in following that bad example? Because they have passed personal-liberty bills, and have, to that extent, violated the compact which is reciprocal, shall we turn round, on the other hand, and violate the Constitution by coercing them to a compliance with it? Will we do so?

"Then I come back to the starting point: let us stand in the Union and upon the Constitution; and if anybody is to leave this Union, or violate its guaranties, it shall be those who have taken the initiative, and passed their personal-liberty bills. I am in the Union, and intend to stay in it. I intend to hold on to the Union, and the guaranties under which this Union has grown; and I do not intend to be driven from it, nor out of it, by their unconstitutional enactments.

"Then, Mr. President, suppose, for instance, that a fugitive is arrested in the State of Vermont to-morrow, and under the personal-liberty bill of that State, or the law—I do not remember its precise title now—which prevents, or is intended to prevent, the faithful execution of the fugitive-slave law, Vermont undertakes to rescue him, and prevent the enforcement of the law: what is it? It is nullification; it is resistance to the laws of the United States made in conformity with the Constitution; it is rebellion; and it is the duty of the President of the United States to enforce the law, at all hazards and to the last extremity. And if the Federal Government fails or refuses to execute the laws made in conformity with the Constitution, and those States persist in their violation and let those unconstitutional acts remain upon their statute-books, and carry them into practice; if the Government, on the one hand, fails to execute the laws of the United States, and those States, by their enactments, violate them on the other, the Government is at an end, and the parties are all released from the compact

* * * * *

"I think it will be determined by the courts and by the judgment of the country, that the acts passed in 1850 and 1858 by the Legislature of Vermont are a violation, a gross, palpable violation of the Constitution of the United States. It is clear and conclusive to my mind, that a State passing an unconstitutional act, intended to impede or to prevent the execution of a law passed by the Congress of the United States which is constitutional, is thereby placed, so far as the initiative is concerned, in a state of rebellion. It is an open act of nullification. I am not aware that there has been any attempt in Vermont to wrest any persons out of the hands of the officers of the United States, or to imprison or to fine any person under the operation of this law; but the passage of such an act is to initiate rebellion. I think it comes in conflict directly with the spirit and letter of the Constitution of the United States, and to that extent is an act of nullification, and places the State in open rebellion to the United States.

* * * * *

"President Washington thought there was power

in this Government to execute its laws; he considered the militia the army of the Constitution; and he refers to this Union as being inseparable. This is the way that the laws were executed by the Father of his Country, the man who sat as president of the convention that made the Constitution. Here was resistance interposed—opposition to the execution of the laws; and George Washington, then President of the United States, went in person at the head of the militia; and it showed his sagacity, his correct comprehension of men, and the effect that an immediate movement of that kind would have upon them. He ordered fifteen thousand of his countrymen to the scene of action, and went there in person, and stayed there till he was satisfied that the insurrection was quelled. That is the manner in which George Washington put down rebellion. That is the manner in which he executed the laws.

"Here, then, we find General Washington executing the law, in 1795, against a portion of the citizens of Pennsylvania who rebelled; and, I repeat the question, where is the difference between executing the law upon a part and upon the whole? Suppose the whole of Pennsylvania had rebelled and resisted the excise law; had refused to pay taxes on distilleries; was it not as competent and as constitutional for General Washington to have executed the law against the whole as against a part? Is there any difference? Governmental affairs must be practical as well as our own domestic affairs. You may make nice metaphysical distinctions between the practical operations of Government and its theory; you may refine upon what is a State, and point out a difference between a State and a portion of a State; but what is it when you reduce it to practical operation, and square it by common sense?

"In 1832, resistance was interposed to laws of the United States in another State. An ordinance was passed by South Carolina, assuming to act as a sovereign State, to nullify a law of the United States. In 1833, the distinguished man who filled the executive chair, who now lies in his silent grave, loved and respected for his virtue, his honor, his integrity, his patriotism, his undoubted courage, and his devotion to his kind, with an eye single to the promotion of his country's best interests, issued the proclamation, extracts from which I have already presented. He was sworn to support the Constitution, and to see that the laws were faithfully executed; and he fulfilled the obligation. He took all the steps necessary to secure the execution of the law, and he would have executed it by the power of the Government if the point of time had arrived when it was necessary to resort to that power. We can see that he acted upon principles similar to those acted upon by General Washington. He took the precaution of ordering a force there sufficient for the purpose of enabling him to say effectually to the rebellious, and those who were interposing opposition to the execution of the laws, 'The laws which are made according to the Constitution, the laws that provide for the collection of the revenue to sustain this Government, must be enforced, and the revenue must be collected. It is a part of the compact; it is a part of the engagement you have undertaken to perform, and you of your own will have no power or authority to set it aside.' The duties were collected; the law was enforced; and the Government went on. In his proclamation he made a powerful appeal. He told them what would be done; and it would have been done, as certain as God rules on high, if the time had arrived which made it necessary.

"Then we see where General Washington stood, and where General Jackson stood. Now, how does the present case stand? The time has come when men should speak out. Duties are mine; consequences are God's. I intend to discharge my duty, and I intend to avow my understanding of the Constitution and the laws of the country. Have we no authority or power to execute the laws in the State of South Carolina as well as in Vermont and Pennsylvania? I think we have. As I before said, although a State may, by an ordinance, or by a resolve, or by an act of any other kind, declare that they absolve their citizens from all allegiance to this Government, it does not release them from the compact. The compact is reciprocal; and they, in coming into it, undertook to perform certain duties and abide by the laws made in conformity with the compact. Now, sir, what is the Government to do in South Carolina? If South Carolina undertakes to drive the Federal courts out of that State, the Federal Government has the right to hold those courts there. She may attempt to exclude the mails, yet the Federal Government has the right to establish post-offices and post-roads, and to carry the mails there. She may resist the collection of revenue at Charleston, or any other point that the Government has provided for its collection; but the Government has the right to collect it and to enforce the law. She may undertake to take possession of the property belonging to the Government, which was originally ceded by the State, but the Federal Government has the right to provide the means for retaining possession of that property. If she makes an advance either to dispossess the Government of that which it has purchased, or to resist the execution of the revenue laws, or of our judicial system, or the carrying of the mails, or the exercise of any other power conferred on the Federal Government, she puts herself in the wrong, and it will be the duty of the Government to see that the laws are faithfully executed.

* * * * * *

"We are told that certain States will go out and tear this accursed Constitution into fragments, and drag the pillars of this mighty edifice down upon us, and involve us all in one common ruin. Will the Border States submit to such a threat? No. But if they do not come into the movement, the pillars of this stupendous fabric of human freedom and greatness and goodness are to be pulled down, and all will be involved in one common ruin. Such is the threatening language used. 'You shall come into our Confederacy, or we will coerce you to the emancipation of your slaves.' That is the language which is held towards us.

"There are many ideas afloat about this threatened dissolution, and it is time to speak out. The question arises, in reference to the protection and preservation of the institution of slavery, whether dissolution is a remedy, or will give to it protection. I avow here, to-day, that if I were an Abolitionist, and wanted to accomplish the overthrow and abolition of the institution of slavery in the Southern States, the first step that I would take would be to break the bonds of this Union, and dissolve this Government. I believe the continuance of slavery depends upon the preservation of this Union, and a compliance with all the guaranties of the Constitution. I believe an interference with it will break up the Union; and I believe a dissolution of the Union will, in the end, though it may be some time to come, overthrow the institution of slavery. Hence we find so many in the North who desire the dissolution of these States, as the most certain, and direct, and effectual means of overthrowing the institution of slavery.

"What protection would it be to us to dissolve this Union? What protection would it be to us to convert this nation into two hostile powers, the one warring with the other? Whose property is at stake? Whose interest is endangered? Is it not the property of the border States? Suppose Canada were moved down upon our border, and the two separated sections, then different nations, were hostile: what would the institution of slavery be worth on the border? Every man who has common sense will see that the institution would take up its march and retreat, as certainly and as unerringly as general laws can operate. Yes; it would commence to retreat the very moment this Union was divided into two hostile powers, and you made the line between the slaveholding and non-slaveholding States the line of division.

"Then, what remedy do we get for the institution of slavery? Must we keep up a standing army?

Must we keep up forts bristling with arms along the whole border? This is a question to be considered, one that involves the future; and no step should be taken without mature reflection. Before this Union is dissolved and broken up, we in Tennessee, as one of the Slave States, want to be consulted; we want to know what protection we are to have; whether we are simply to be made outposts and guards to protect the property of others, at the same time that we sacrifice and lose our own. We want to understand this question.

"Again: if there is one division of the States, will there not be more than one? I heard a senator say, the other day, that he would rather see this Government separated into thirty-three fractional parts than to see it consolidated; but when you once begin to divide, when the first division is made, who can tell when the next will be made? When these States are all turned loose, and a different condition of things is presented, with complex and abstruse interests to be considered, and weighed, and understood, what combinations may take place no one can tell. I am opposed to the consolidation of government, and I am as much for the reserved rights of States as any one; but, rather than see this Union divided into thirty-three petty governments, with a little prince in one, a potentate in another, a little aristocracy in a third, a little democracy in a fourth, and a republic somewhere else; a citizen not being able to pass from one State to another without a passport or a commission from his government; with quarrelling and warring amongst the little petty powers, which would result in anarchy; I would rather see this Government to-day—I proclaim it here in my place—converted into a consolidated government. It would be better for the American people; it would be better for our kind; it would be better for humanity; better for Christianity; better for all that tends to elevate and ennoble man, than breaking up this splendid, this magnificent, this stupendous fabric of human government, the most perfect that the world ever saw, and which has succeeded thus far without a parallel in the history of the world.

* * * * * *

"I throw these out as considerations. There will be various projects and various combinations made. Memphis is now connected with Norfolk, in the Old Dominion; Memphis is connected with Baltimore within two days. Here is a coast that lets us out to the commerce of the world. When we look around in the four States of Tennessee, Kentucky, Virginia, and Maryland, there are things about which our memories, our attachments, and our associations linger with pride and pleasure. Go down into the Old Dominion; there is the place where, in 1781, Cornwallis surrendered his sword to the immortal Washington. In the bosom of her soil are deposited her greatest and best sons. Move along in that trail, and there we find Jefferson, and Madison, and Monroe, and a long list of worthies.

"We come next to old North Carolina, my native State, God bless her! She is my mother. Though she was not my cherishing mother, to use the language of the classics, she is the mother whom I love, and I cling to her with undying affection, as a son should cling to an affectionate mother. We find

Macon, who was associated with our early history, deposited in her soil. Go to King's Mountain, on her borders, and you there find the place on which the battle was fought that turned the tide of the Revolution. Yes, within her borders the signal battle was fought that turned the tide which resulted in the surrender of Cornwallis at Yorktown, in the Old Dominion.

"Travel on a little further, and we get back to Tennessee. I shall be as modest as I can in reference to her, but she has some associations that make her dear to the people of the United States. In Tennessee we have our own illustrious Jackson. There he sleeps —that Jackson who issued his proclamation in 1833, and saved this Government. We have our Polk and our Grundy, and a long list of others who are worthy of remembrance.

"And who lie in Kentucky? Your Hardings, your Boones, your Roanes, your Clays, are among the dead; your CRITTENDEN among the living. All are identified and associated with the history of the country.

"Maryland has her Carroll of Carrollton, and a long list of worthies, who are embalmed in the hearts of the American people. And you are talking about breaking up this Republic, with this cluster of associations, these ties of affection, around you. May we not expect that some means may be devised by which it can be held together?

"Here, too, in the centre of the Republic, is the seat of government, which was founded by Washington, and bears his immortal name. Who dare appropriate it exclusively? It is within the borders of the States I have enumerated, in whose limits are found the graves of Washington, of Jackson, of Polk, of Clay. From them is it supposed that we will be torn away? No, sir; we will cherish these endearing associations with the hope, if this Republic shall be broken, that we may speak words of peace and reconciliation to a distracted, a divided, I may add, a maddened people. Angry waves may be lashed into fury on the one hand; on the other blustering winds may rage; but we stand immovable upon our basis, as on our own native mountains—presenting their craggy brows, their unexplored caverns, their summits 'rock-ribbed, and ancient as the sun,'—we stand speaking peace, association, and concert to a distracted Republic.

"But, Mr. President, will it not be well, before we break up this great Government, to inquire what kind of a government this new government in the South is to be, with which we are threatened unless we involve our destinies with this rash and precipitate movement? What intimation is there in reference to its character? Before my State and those States of which I have been speaking, go into a Southern or Northern confederacy, ought they not to have some idea of the kind of government that is to be formed? What are the intimations in the South in reference to the formation of a new government? The language of some speakers is, that they want a Southern government obliterating all State lines—a government of consolidation. It is alarming and distressing to entertain the proposition here. What ruin and disaster would follow, if we are to have a consolidated government here! But the idea is afloat and current in the South that a Southern government is to be established, in the language of some of the speakers in the State of Georgia, 'obliterating all State lines.' Is that the kind of entertainment to which the people are to be invited? Is that the kind of government under which we are to pass; and are we to be forced to emancipate our slaves unless we go into it? Another suggestion in reference to a Southern government is, that we shall have a Southern Confederacy of great strength and power, with a constitutional provision preventing any State from changing its domestic institutions without the consent of three-fourths, or some great number to be fixed upon. Is that the kind of government under which we want to pass? I avow here, that, so far as I am concerned, I will never enter, with my consent, any government, North or South, less republican, less democratic, than the one under which we now live.

* * * * *

"If there are grievances, why cannot we all go together, and write them down, and point them out to our Northern friends, after we have agreed on what those grievances are, and say: 'Here is what we demand; here our wrongs are enumerated; upon these terms we have agreed; and now, after we have given you a reasonable time to consider these additional guaranties in order to protect ourselves against these wrongs, if you refuse them, then, having made an honorable effort, having exhausted all other means, we may declare the association to be broken up, and we may go into an act of revolution.' We can then say to them: 'You have refused to give us guaranties that we think are needed for the protection of our institutions and for the protection of our other interests.' When they do this, I will go as far as he who goes the furthest.

"I tell them here to-day, if they do not do it, Tennessee will be found standing as firm and unyielding in her demands for those guaranties, in the way a State should stand, as any other State in this Confederacy. She is not quite so belligerent now. She is not making quite so much noise. She is not as blustering as Sempronius was in the council in Addison's play of 'Cato,' who declared that his 'voice was still for war.' There was another character there, Lucius, who was called upon to state what his opinions were ; and he replied that he must confess his thoughts were turned on peace ; but when the extremity came, Lucius, who was deliberative, who was calm, and whose thoughts were upon peace, was found true to the interests of his country. He proved himself to be a man and a soldier ; while the other was a traitor and a coward. We will do our duty ; we will stand upon principle, and defend it to the last extremity.

"We do not think, though, that we have just cause for going out of the Union now. We have just cause of complaint ; but we are for remaining in the Union, and fighting the battle like men. We do not intend to be cowardly, and turn our backs on our own camps. We intend to stay and fight the battle here upon this consecrated ground. Why should we retreat? Because Mr. Lincoln has been elected President of the United States? Is this any cause why we should retreat? Does not every man, senator or otherwise, know, that if Mr. Breckinridge had been elected we should not be to-day for dissolving the Union? Then what is the issue? It is because we have not got our man. If we had got our man, we should not have been for breaking up the Union; but as Mr. Lincoln is elected, we are for breaking up the Union! I say no. Let us show ourselves men, and men of courage.

"How has Mr. Lincoln been elected, and how have Mr. Breckinridge and Mr. Douglas been defeated? By the votes of the American people, cast according to the Constitution and the forms of law, though it has been upon a sectional issue. It is not the first time in our history that two candidates have been elected from the same section of country. General Jackson and Mr. Calhoun were elected on the same ticket; but nobody considered that cause of dissolution. They were from the South. I oppose the sectional spirit that has produced the election of Lincoln and Hamlin, yet it has been done according to the Constitution and according to the forms of law. I believe we have the power in our own hands, and I am not willing to shrink from the responsibility of exercising that power.

"How has Lincoln been elected, and upon what basis does he stand? A minority President by nearly a million votes; but had the election taken place upon the plan proposed in my amendment of the Constitution, by districts, he would have been this day defeated. But it has been done according to the Constitution and according to law. I am for abiding by the Constitution; and in abiding by it I want to maintain and retain my place here, and put down Mr. Lincoln, and drive back his advances upon

Southern institutions, if he designs to make any. Have we not got the brakes in our hands? Have we not got the power? We have. Let South Carolina send her senators back; let all the senators come; and on the fourth of March next we shall have a majority of six in this body against him. This successful sectional candidate, who is in a minority of a million, or nearly so, on the popular vote, cannot make his Cabinet on the fourth of March next, unless the Senate will permit him.

"Am I to be so great a coward as to retreat from duty? I will stand here and meet the encroachments upon the institutions of my country at the threshold; and as a man, as one that loves my country and my constituents, I will stand here and resist all encroachments and advances. Here is the place to stand. Shall I desert the citadel, and let the enemy come in and take possession? No. Can Mr. Lincoln send a foreign minister, or even a consul, abroad, unless he receives the sanction of the Senate? Can he appoint a postmaster whose salary is over a thousand dollars a year without the consent of the Senate? Shall we desert our posts, shrink from our responsibilities, and permit Mr. Lincoln to come with his cohorts, as we consider them, from the North, to carry off every thing? Are we so cowardly that now that we are defeated, not conquered, we shall do this? Yes, we are defeated according to the forms of law and the Constitution; but the real victory is ours—the moral force is with us. Are we going to desert that noble and that patriotic band who have stood by us at the North, who have stood by us upon principle, and upon the Constitution?

They stood by us, and fought the battle upon principle; and now that we have been defeated, not conquered, are we to turn our backs upon them and leave them to their fate? I, for one, will not. I intend to stand by them. How many votes did we get in the North? We got more votes in the North against Lincoln than the entire Southern States cast. Are they not able and faithful allies? They are; and now, on account of this temporary defeat, are we to turn our backs upon them and leave them to their fate?

"We find, when all the North is summed up, that Mr. Lincoln's majority there is only about two hundred thousand on the popular vote; and when that is added to the other vote cast throughout the Union, he stands to-day in a minority of nearly a million votes. What, then, is necessary to be done? To stand to our posts like men, and act upon principle; stand for the country; and in four years from this day, Lincoln and his administration will be turned out—the worst-defeated and broken-down party that ever came into power. It is an inevitable result from the combination of elements that now exist. What cause, then, is there to break up the Union? What reason is there for deserting our posts, and destroying this greatest and best government that was ever spoken into existence?

"I voted against him; I spoke against him; I spent my money to defeat him;—but still I love my country; I love the Constitution; I intend to insist upon its guaranties. There, and there alone, I intend to plant myself, with the confident hope and belief that if the Union remains together, in less than four years the now triumphant party will be overthrown. In less time, I have the hope and belief that we shall unite and agrèe upon our grievances here and demand their redress, not as suppliants at the footstool of power, but as parties to a great compact ; we shall say that we want additional guaranties, and that they are necessary to the preservation of this Union ; and then, when they are refused deliberately and calmly, if we cannot do better, let the South go together, and let the North go together, and let us have a division of this Government without the shedding of blood, if such a thing be possible ; let us have a division of the property ; let us have a division of the navy ; let us have a division of the army, and of the public lands. Let it be done in peace, and in a spirit that should characterize and distinguish this people. I believe we can obtain all our guaranties. I believe there is too much good sense, too much intelligence, too much patriotism, too much capability, too much virtue, in the great mass of people to permit this Government to be overthrown.

"I have an abiding faith, I have an unshaken confidence, in man's capability to govern himself. I will not give up this Government that is now called an experiment, which some are prepared to abandon for a constitutional monarchy. No ; I intend to stand by it, and I entreat every man throughout the nation who is a patriot, and who has seen, and is compelled to admit, the success of this great experiment, to come forward, not in heat, not in fanaticism, not in haste, not in precipitancy, but in deliberation, in full view of all that is before us, in the spirit of brotherly love and fraternal affection, and rally around the altar of our common country, and lay the Constitution upon it as our last libation, and swear by our God, and all that is sacred and holy, that the Constitution shall be saved and the Union preserved. Yes, in the language of the departed Jackson, let us exclaim that the Union, 'the Federal Union, it must be preserved.'

"Are we likely, when we get to ourselves, North and South, to sink into brotherly love? Are we likely to be as harmonious in that condition as some suppose? I am sometimes impressed with the force of Mr. Jefferson's remark, that we may as well keep the North to quarrel with; for if we have no North to quarrel with, we shall quarrel among ourselves. We are a sort of quarrelsome, pugnacious people; and if we cannot get a quarrel from one quarter, we shall have it from another; and I would rather quarrel a little now with the North than be quarrelling with ourselves. What did a senator say here in the American Senate, only a few days ago, because the governor of a Southern State was refusing to convene the Legislature to hasten this movement that was going on throughout the South, and because he objected to that course of conduct? The question was asked, if there was not some Texan Brutus that would rise up and rid the country of the hoary-headed traitor! This is the language that a senator used. This is the way we begin to speak of Southern governors. Yes; to remove an obstacle in our way, we must have a modern Brutus, who will go to the capital of a State and assassinate a governor to accelerate the movement. If we are so unscrupulous in reference to ourselves, and in reference to the means we are willing to employ to consummate this dissolution, then it does not look very much like harmony among ourselves after we get out of it.

"Mr. President, I have said much more than I anticipated when I commenced, and I have spoken more at length than a regard for my own health and strength would have allowed ; but if there is any effort of mine that would preserve this Government till there is time to think, till there is time to consider, even if it cannot be preserved any longer ; if that end could be secured by making a sacrifice of my existence and offering up my blood, I would be willing to consent to it. Let us pause in this mad career; let us hesitate. Let us consider well what we are doing before we make a movement. I believe that, to a certain extent, dissolution is going to take place. I say to the North, you ought to come up in the spirit which should characterize and control the North on this question; and you ought to give those indications of good faith that will approach what the South demands. It will be no sacrifice on your part. It is no suppliancy on ours, but simply a demand of right. What concession is there in doing right? Then, come forward. We have it in our power—yes, this Congress here to-day has it in its power to save this Union, even after South Carolina has gone out. Will they not do it? You can do it. Who is willing to take the dreadful alternative without making an honorable effort to save this Government? This Congress has it in its power to-day to arrest this thing, at least for a season, until there is time to consider about it, until we can act discreetly and prudently, and I believe arrest it altogether.

"Shall we give all this up to the Vandals and the Goths? Shall we shrink from our duty, and desert the Government as a sinking ship, or shall we stand by it? I, for one, will stand here until the high behest of my constituents demands of me to desert my post; and instead of laying hold of the columns of this fabric and pulling it down, though I may not be much of a prop, I will stand with my shoulder supporting the edifice as long as human effort can do it.

"In saying what I have said on this occasion, Mr. President, I have had in view the duty that I owe to my constituents, to my children, to myself. Without regard to consequences, I have taken my position; and when the tug comes, when Greek shall meet Greek, and our rights are refused after all honorable means have been exhausted, then it is that I will perish in the last breach; yes, in the language of the patriot Emmet, 'I will dispute every inch of ground; I will burn every blade of grass; and the last intrenchment of Freedom shall be my grave.' Then, let us stand by the Constitution; and in preserving the Constitution we shall save the Union; and in saving the Union, we save this the greatest Government on earth."

CHAPTER II.

THE HOMESTEAD BILL.

THE great triumph of President Johnson's congressional career is his advocacy and ultimately successful championship of the famous Homestead Bill. Thoughtful men had for years seen the evil and condemned the policy of selling the public domain in large sections to speculators and monopolists, who merely held them for their private and selfish gains. This feeling eventuated in the formation of the Land Reform Association, whose headquarters were in the city of New York, with branches in various portions of the country. This society, whose organ was a very ably conducted weekly paper, called Young America, endeavored to enlighten the public mind, and arouse the popular sentiment in relation to the curse of land monopoly, and to point out an easy and beneficent cure for the great and growing evil. The plan recommended was to donate the public lands to actual settlers in limited quantities, upon condition of real residence, improvement, and cultivation. This system, argued its advocates, would promote the growth of a landed democracy, founded upon the possession and improvement of a homestead, and forming the firmest support of a free government, and the surest base of republican institutions.

Documents and papers urging this great and patriotic policy upon public consideration were forwarded to all members of the Federal Congress, but upon no one did it make the impression produced upon the clear intellect, far-seeing statesmanship, and purely Democratic proclivities of Andrew Johnson. He immediately made himself its especial champion, and fighting its battle with characteristic courage, perseverance, and ability, against great and bitter opposition, he finally, after a struggle of twelve long years, carried it through in triumph, and it is to-day diffusing its blessings over the roofs and hearthstones of thousands of contented and happy families.

The speech of President Johnson upon the Homestead Bill, delivered in the Senate, May 20th, 1858, is so full of elevated statesmanship, and so clear and powerful an exposition of the entire merits of the question, that we give it to our readers entire, for no abstract or analysis can be made of its arguments and illustrations, without failing in justice to its compact and forcible arrangement.

"Mr. President—The immediate proposition before the Senate is an amendment offered by the honorable senator from North Carolina,* which provides that there shall be a land-warrant issued to each head of a family, by the Secretary of the Interior, and distributed among those who do not emigrate to the public domain, and take possession of and cultivate the land for the term of years specified in the bill. I have something to say in reference to that amendment, but I will not say it in this connection. I will take it up in its order. I propose, in the first place, to explain briefly the provisions of the bill.

"The first section provides for granting one hundred and sixty acres of land to every head of a family who will emigrate to any of the public domain and settle upon it, and cultivate it for a term of five years. Upon those facts being made known to the register of the land-office, the emigrant is to be entitled to obtain a patent. The second section provides that he shall make an affidavit, and show to the satisfaction of the officer that his entry is made in good faith, and that his intention is to cultivate the soil and become an actual settler. The sixth section of the bill provides that any person who is now an inhabitant of the United States, but not a citizen, if he makes application, and in the course of five years becomes a citizen of the United States, shall be placed on a footing of equality with the native-born citizens of the country in this respect. The third section provides that those entries shall be confined to land that has been in market, and subjected to private entry; and that the persons entering the land shall be confined to each alternate section.

* Mr. Clingman.

"These are substantially the leading provisions of this bill. It does not proceed upon the idea, as some suppose, of making a donation or gift of the public land to the settler. It proceeds upon the principle of consideration; and I conceive, and I think many others do, that the individual who emigrates to the West, and reclaims and reduces to cultivation one hundred and sixty acres of the public domain, subjecting himself to all the privations and hardships of such a life, pays the highest consideration for his land.

"But, before I say more on this portion of the subject, I desire to premise a little by giving the history of this homestead proposition. Some persons from my own region of the country, or, in other words, from the South, have thrown out the intimation that this is a proposition which partakes, to some extent, of the nature of the Emigrant Aid Society, and is to operate injuriously to the Southern States. For the purpose of making the starting-point right, I want to go back and show when this proposition was first introduced into the Congress of the United States. I am not sure but that the Presiding Officer* remembers well the history of this measure.

"In 1846, on the 27th day of March, long before we had any emigrant aid societies, long before we had the compromises of 1850 in reference to the slavery question, long before we had any agitation on the subject of slavery in 1854, long before we had any agitation upon it in 1858, this proposition made its advent into the House of Representatives. It met with considerable opposition. It scarcely received serious

* Mr. Foot, of Vermont, in the chair.

consideration for a length of time; but the measure was pressed until the public mind took hold of it; and it was still pressed until the 12th day of May, 1852, when it passed that body by a two-thirds vote. Thus we see that its origin and its consummation, so far as the House of Representatives was concerned, had nothing to do with North or South, but proceeded upon that great principle which interests every man in this country, and which, in the end, secures and provides for him a home. By putting these dates together, it will be perceived that it was just six years, five months, and fifteen days from the introduction of this bill until its passage by the House of Representatives.

"I shall not detain the Senate by any lengthy remarks on the general principles of the bill; for I do not intend to be prolix, or to consume much of the Senate's time. What is the origin of the great idea of a homestead of land? We find, on turning to the first law-writer—and I think one of the best, for we are informed that he wrote by inspiration—that he advances the first idea on this subject. Moses made use of the following language:

"'The land shall not be sold forever; for the land is mine—for ye are strangers and sojourners with me.'—*Leviticus*, xxv. 23.

"We begin, then, with Moses. The next writer to whom I will call the attention of the Senate is Vattel—one of the ablest, if not the ablest writer upon the laws of nations. He lays down this great principle:*

"'Of all the arts, tillage or agriculture is the most

* Vattel, Book I. ch. 7.

useful and necessary. It is the nursing-father of the State. The cultivation of the earth causes it to produce an infinite increase; it forms the surest resource, and the most solid fund of rich commerce for the people who enjoy a happy climate.

"'This affair, then, deserves the utmost attention from Government. The sovereign ought to neglect no means of rendering the land under his obedience as well cultivated as possible. He ought not to allow either communities or private persons to acquire large tracts of land to leave uncultivated. These rights of common, which deprive the proprietor of the free liberty of disposing of his lands—that will not allow him to farm them, and cause them to be cultivated in the most advantageous manner—these rights, I say, are contrary to the welfare of the State, and ought to be suppressed or reduced to a just bound. The property introduced among the citizens does not prevent the nation's having a right to take the most effectual measures to cause the whole country to produce the greatest and most advantageous revenue possible.

"'The Government ought carefully to avoid every thing capable of discouraging husbandmen, or of diverting them from the labors of agriculture. Those taxes, those excessive and ill-proportioned impositions, the burden of which falls almost entirely upon the cultivators, and the vexations they suffer from the commissioners who levy them, take from the unhappy peasant the means of cultivating the earth, and depopulate the country. Spain is the most fertile and the worst cultivated country in Europe. The Church possesses too much land, and the undertakers of royal magazines, who are authorized to purchase at low prices all the corn they find in possession of a peasant, above what is necessary for the subsistence of his wife and family, so greatly discourage the husbandman, that he sows no more corn than is necessary for the support of his own household. Whence arises the greatest scarcity in a country capable of feeding its neighbors.

"'Another abuse injurious to agriculture is, the contempt cast upon husbandmen. The inhabitants of cities, even the most servile artist and the most lazy citizen, consider him who cultivates the soil with a disdainful eye; they humble and discourage him; they dare to despise a profession that feeds the human race—the natural employment of man. A stay-maker places far beneath him the beloved employment of the first consuls and dictators of Rome.

"'China has wisely prevented this abuse. Agriculture is there held in honor; and to preserve this happy manner of thinking, every year, on a solemn day, the Emperor himself, followed by the whole court, sets his hands to the plough and sows a small piece of land. Hence China is the best cultivated country in the world. It nourishes an innumerable multitude of people that at first appears to the traveller too great for the space they possess.

"'The cultivation of the soil is not only to be recommended by the Government on account of the extraordinary advantages that flow from it, but from its being an obligation imposed by nature on mankind. The whole earth is appointed for the nourishment of its inhabitants, but it would be incapable of doing it was it uncultivated. Every nation is then obliged by a law of nature to cultivate the ground that has fallen to its share, and it has no right to expect or require assistance from others, any further than the land in its possession is incapable of furnishing it with necessaries. Those people, like the ancient Germans and modern Tartars, who, having fertile countries, disdain to cultivate the earth, and rather choose to live by rapine, are wanting to themselves, and deserve to be exterminated as savage and rapacious beasts. There are others who avoid agriculture, who would only live by hunting and flocks. This might doubtless be allowed in the first ages of the world, when the earth produced more than was sufficient to feed its few inhabitants; but at present, when the human race is so greatly multiplied, it would not subsist if all nations resolved to live in this manner. Those who still retain this idle life usurp more extensive territories than they would have occasion for were they to use honest labor, and have, therefore, no reason to complain if other nations, more laborious and too closely confined, come to possess a part. Thus, though the conquest of the civilized empires of Peru and Mexico was a notorious usurpation, the establishment of many colonies in North America may, on their confining themselves within just bounds, be extremely lawful. The people of those vast countries rather overran than inhabited them.'

"I propose next to cite the authority of General Jackson, who was believed to be not only a friend to the South but a friend to the Union. He inculcated this great doctrine in his message of 1832:

"'It cannot be doubted that the speedy settlement

of those lands constitutes the true interest of the Republic. The wealth and strength of a country are its population, and the best part of the population are cultivators of the soil. Independent farmers are everywhere the basis of society, and the true friends of liberty.'

* * * * *

"'It seems to me to be our true policy that the public lands shall cease, as soon as practicable, to be a source of revenue; and that they be sold to settlers in limited parcels, at prices barely sufficient to reimburse the United States the expense of the present system, and the cost arising from our Indian contracts.'

* * * * *

"'It is desirable, however, that the right of the soil, and the future disposition of it, be surrendered to the States respectively in which it lies.

"'The adventurous and hardy population of the West, besides contributing their equal share of taxation under the impost system, have, in the progress of our Government, for the lands they occupy, paid into the treasury a large proportion of forty million dollars, and of the revenue received therefrom but a small portion has been expended among them. When, to the disadvantage of their situation in this respect, we add the consideration that it is their labor alone that gives real value to the lands, and that the proceeds arising from these sales are chiefly distributed among States that had not originally any claim to them, and which have enjoyed the undivided emoluments arising from the sales of their own lands, it cannot be expected that the new States will remain longer contented with the present policy, after the payment of the public debt. To avert the consequences which may be apprehended from this cause, to stop forever all partial and interested legislation on this subject, and to afford every American citizen of enterprise the opportunity of securing an independent freehold, it seems to me, therefore, best to abandon the idea of raising a future revenue out of the public lands.'

"Thus we have standing before us, in advocacy of this great principle, the first writer of laws, Moses; next we have Vattel; and in the third place we have General Jackson.

"Now, let us see whether there has been any homestead policy in the United States. By turning to our statutes, we find that the first homestead bill ever introduced into the Congress of the United States was in 1791. I know that it is said by some, and it is sometimes cantingly and slurringly reiterated in the newspapers, that this is a demagogical movement, and that some person has introduced and advocates this policy purely for the purpose of pleasing the people. I want to see who some of these demagogues are; and, before I read the section of this statute, I will refer, in connection with Jackson and those other distinguished individuals, to the fact that Mr. Jefferson, the philosopher and statesman, recognized and appreciated this great doctrine. In 1791, the first bill passed by the Congress of the United States recognizing the homestead principle, is in the following words:

"'That four hundred acres of land be given'—
that is the language of the statute. We do not assume in this bill to give land. We assume that a

consideration passes ; but here was a law that was based on the idea that four hundred acres of land were to be given

—" 'to each of those persons who, in the year 1783, were heads of families at Vincennes, or the Illinois country, or the Mississippi, and who, since that time, have removed from one of the said places to the other; but the Governor of the Territory northwest of the Ohio is hereby directed to cause the same to be laid out for them at their own expense,' etc.

"Another section of the same act provides—

" 'That the heads of families at Vincennes, or in the Illinois country, in the year 1783, who afterwards removed without the limits of said territory, are nevertheless entitled to the donation of four hundred acres of land made by the resolve of Congress,' etc.

"That act recognized the principle embraced in the homestead bill. If this is the idea of a demagogue, if it is the idea of one catering or pandering to the public sentiment to catch votes, it was introduced into Congress in 1791, and received the approval of Washington, the father of his country. I presume that if he lived at this day, and were to approve the measure, as he did in 1791, he would be branded, and put in the category of those persons who are denominated demagogues. Under his administration there was another bill passed of a similar import, recognizing and carrying out the great homestead principle. Thus we find that this policy, so far as legislation is concerned, commenced with Washington, and received his approval as early as 1791. From General Washington's administration there are forty-four precedents, running through every administration of this Government down to the present time, in which this principle has been recognized and indorsed.

"We discover from this historical review that this is no new idea, that it is no recent invention, that it is no new movement for the purpose of making votes; but it is a principle well-nigh as old as the Government itself, which was indorsed and approved by Washington himself.

"This would seem, Mr. President, to settle the question of power. I know it has been argued by some that Congress had not the power to make donations of land; but even the statute to which I have referred makes use of the word 'give,' without consideration. It was considered constitutional by the early fathers to give away land. We proceed in this bill upon the principle that there is a consideration. If I were disposed to look for precedents, even for the donations of the public lands, I could instance the bounty-land act, I could take you through other acts donating land, showing that the principle has been recognized again and again, and that there is not now a question as to its constitutionality.

"I believe there is a clear difference in the power of the Federal Government in reference to its appropriations of money and its appropriations of the public land. The Congress of the United States has power to lay and collect taxes, duties, imposts, and excises, to pay the debts and provide for the common defence and general welfare. I believe it has the power to lay and collect duties for these legitimate purposes; but when taxes have been laid, collected, and paid into the treasury, I do not think it has that general scope or that latitude in the appropriation of money that it has over the public lands. Once converted into revenue, Congress can only appropriate the revenue to the specific objects of the Constitution. It may derive revenue from the public lands, and being revenue, it can only be appropriated to the purposes for which revenue is raised under the Constitution.

"But when we turn to another provision of the Constitution, we find that Congress has power 'to dispose of and make all needful rules and regulations respecting the territory or other property belonging to the United States.' Congress has, in the organization of all the Territories and in the admission of new States, recognized most clearly the principle of appropriating the public lands for the benefit of schools, colleges, and academies. It has granted the sixteenth and thirty-sixth sections of every township for school purposes ; it has granted lands for public buildings and various other improvements. I am very clear on this point, that in the disposition of the public lands they should be applied to national purposes. If we grant the public lands to actual settlers, so as to induce them to settle upon and cultivate them, can there be any thing more national in its character? What is the great object of acquiring territory? Is it not for settlement and cultivation? We may acquire territory by the exercise of the treaty-making power. We may be engaged in a war, and as terms or conditions of peace we may make large acquisitions of territory to the United States. But what is the great idea and principle on which you acquire territory? Is it not to settle and cultivate it?

"I am aware that the argument is used, if you can

dispose of the public lands for this purpose or that purpose, cannot you sell the public lands and apply the proceeds to the same purpose? I think there is a clear distinction between the two cases. It is equally clear to me that, if the Federal Government can set apart the public lands for school purposes in the new States, it can appropriate lands to enable the parent to sustain the child whilst enjoying the benefits conferred upon him by the Government in the shape of education. The argument is as sound in the one case as it is in the other. If we can grant lands in the one case, we can in the other. If, without making a contract in advance, you can grant your public lands as gratuities, as donations to men who go out and fight the battles of their country, after the services have been rendered, is it not strange, passing strange, that you cannot grant land to those who till the soil and make provision to sustain your army while it is fighting the battles of the country? It seems to me that the argument is clear. I do not intend to argue the constitutional question, for I think there can be really no doubt on that point. I do not believe any one at this day will seriously make any point on that ground against this bill. Is its purpose a national one? The great object is to induce persons to cultivate the land, and thereby make the soil productive. By doing this, you induce hundreds of persons throughout the United States, who are now producing but little, to come in contact with the soil and add to the productive capacity of the country, and thereby promote the national weal.

"I come now to the amendment offered by the senator from North Carolina. I have not looked over the

Globe this morning to read his remarks of yesterday; but if I understood him correctly, he advocated the proposition of issuing a warrant for a hundred and sixty acres of land to each head of a family in the United States. I am inclined to think the senator is not serious in this proposition. It has been offered on some occasions heretofore, and rejected by very decided votes. Let us compare it with the proposition of the bill. The idea of the honorable senator seems to be that this bill was designed to force or compel, to some extent, the citizens of other States to go to the new States. Why, sir, there is no compulsory process in the bill. It leaves each man at his own discretion, at his own free will, either to go or to stay, just as it suits his inclinations.

"The senator seems to think too—and the same idea was advanced by his predecessor—that at this time such a measure would have a tendency to diminish the revenue. He intimates that the nation is now bankrupt, that we are borrowing money, that the receipts from customs have been greatly diminished, and that therefore it would be dangerous to pass this bill, because it would have a tendency to diminish the revenue. Let us compare the senator's proposition and that of the bill, in this respect. His amendment is to issue warrants to each head of a family. The population of the United States is now estimated at about twenty-eight millions. Let us assume, for the sake of illustration, that there are three million heads of families in the United States. His proposition, then, is to issue and throw upon the market three millions of warrants, each warrant entitling the holder to one hundred and sixty acres of land. If that were done, and those warrants were thrown upon the market, what would they sell for? Little or nothing. If such land-warrants were thrown broadcast over the country, who would enter another acre of land at $1.25? Would not the warrants pass into the hands of land-speculators and monopolists at a merely nominal price? Would they bring more than a quarter of a dollar an acre? If you were to throw three millions of land-warrants into the market at one time, would they bring any thing? Then the effect of that proposition would be to do but little good to those to whom the warrants were issued; and by throwing them into the market, it would cut off the revenue from public lands entirely, for no one would enter land for cash as long as warrants could be bought. That proposition, then, is to aid and feed speculation. I do not say that is the motive or intention, but it is the tendency and effect of the senator's proposition to throw a large portion of the public lands into the hands of speculators, and to cut them off from the treasury as a source of revenue.

"But what does this bill propose? Will it diminish the receipts into the treasury from the public lands? The bill provides that the entries under it shall be confined to the alternate sections, and that the person who obtains the benefit of the bill must be an actual settler and cultivator. In proportion as you settle and cultivate any portion of the public lands, do you not enhance the value of the remaining sections, and bring them into the market much sooner, and obtain a better price for them than you would without this bill? What is the principle upon which you have proceeded in all the railroad grants you have made? They have been defended upon the ground that by granting alternate sections for railroads, you thereby brought the remaining lands into the market, and enabled the Government to realize its means at a much earlier period, making the remainder of the public lands more valuable than they were before. This bill proceeds upon the same idea. You have granted an immense amount of lands to railroads on this principle, and now why not do something for the people?

"I say, that instead of wasting the public lands, instead of reducing the receipts into the treasury, this bill would increase them. In the first place, it will enhance the value of the reserved quarter-sections. This may be illustrated by an example. In 1848 we had nine million quarter-sections; in 1858 we have about seven millions. Let us suppose that our population is twenty-eight millions, and that under the operation of this bill one million heads of families who are now producing but very little, and who have no land to cultivate, and very scanty means of subsistence, shall each have a quarter-section of land, what will the effect be? At present these persons pay little or nothing for the support of the Federal Government, under the operation of our tariff system, for the reason that they have not got much to buy with. How much does the land yield to the Government while it is lying in a state of nature, uncultivated? Nothing at all. At the rate we have been selling the public lands, about three million dollars' worth a year, estimating them at $1.25 an acre, it will take a fraction less than seven hundred years to dispose of the public domain.

"I will take a case that will demonstrate as clearly as the simplest sum in arithmetic that this is a revenue measure. Let us take a million families who can now hardly procure the necessaries of life, and place them each on a quarter-section of land,—how long will it be before their condition will be improved so as to make them able to contribute something to the support of the Government? Now, here is soil producing nothing, here are hands producing but little. Transfer the man from the point where he is producing nothing, bring him in contact with a hundred and sixty acres of productive soil, and how long will it be before that man changes his condition? As soon as he gets upon the land he begins to make his improvements, he clears out his field, and the work of production is commenced. In a short time he has a crop, he has stock and other things that result from bringing his physical labor in contact with the soil. He has the products of his labor and his land, and he is enabled to exchange them for articles of consumption. He is enabled to buy more than he did before, and thus he contributes more to the support of his Government, while, at the same time, he becomes a better man, a more reliable man for all governmental purposes, because he is interested in the country in which he lives.

"To illustrate the matter further, let us take a family of seven persons in number who now have no home, no abiding-place that they can call their own, and transfer them to a tract of one hundred and sixty acres of land which they are to possess and cultivate. Is there a senator here who does not believe, that, by changing their position from one place to the other, they would produce at least a dollar more than they did before? I will begin at a point scarcely visible, —a single dollar. Is there a man here or anywhere else who does not know the fact to be, that you increase a man's ability to buy when he produces more by bringing his labor in contact with the soil. The result of that contact is production; he produces something that he can convert and exchange for the necessities of his family. Suppose the increase was only a dollar a head for a million of families, each family consisting of seven persons. By transferring a million of families from their present dependent condition to the enjoyment and cultivation of the public domain, supposing it would only increase their ability to buy foreign imports to the extent of a dollar each, you would create a demand for seven millions' worth of imports. Our rates of duties, under the tariff act of 1846, are about thirty per cent., and thus, at the almost invisible beginning of a single dollar a head, you, in this way, increase the pecuniary and financial means of the Government to the extent of $2,100,000.

"This would be the result, supposing that there would only be an addition of one dollar per head to the ability of each family, by being taken from a condition of poverty and placed upon one hundred and sixty acres of land. This is the result, supposing them to have seven dollars more, with which to buy articles of consumption, than they had when they had no home, no soil to cultivate, no stimulant, no inducement to labor. If you suppose the effect would be to increase their ability two dollars per head, you would increase their consumption to the amount of $14,000,000, which, at thirty per cent. duty, would yield $4,200,000. If you supposed it increased the ability of a family four dollars per head, the total amount would be $28,000,000, which would yield a revenue of $8,400,000. I think that this would be far below the truth, and if you give a family one hundred and sixty acres of land to cultivate, the effect would be to increase the ability of that family so as to buy fifty-six dollars' worth more than they bought before—eight dollars a head. That would be a small increase to a family who had a home, compared with the condition of that family when it had none. The effect of that would be to run up the amount they buy to $56,000,000, which, at a duty of thirty per cent., would yield the sum of $16,800,000.

"I show you, then, that, by taking one million families, consisting of seven persons each, and putting them each upon a quarter-section of land, making the soil productive, if you thereby only add to their capacity to buy goods to the amount of fifty-six dollars per family, you would derive a revenue of nearly seventeen million dollars. When you have done this, how much of the public lands would you have disposed of? One million quarter-sections, and you would have nearly six million quarter-sections left. By disposing of one-sixth of your public domain in this way, upon this little miniature estimate, you bring into the coffers of the Federal Government by this bill $16,800,000 annually.

"Does this look like diminishing the revenue? Does it not rather show that this bill is a revenue measure? I think it is most clearly a revenue measure. Not only is this the case in a money point of view, so far as the imports are concerned, but, by settling the alternate sections with actual cultivators, you make the remaining sections more valuable to the Government, and you bring them sooner into market. In continuation of this idea, I will read a portion of the argument which I made upon this subject when I first introduced the bill into the other House. I read from the report of my speech on that occasion:

"'Mr. J. said, it will be remembered by the House that he had already shown, that by giving an individual a quarter-section of the land, the Government would receive back, in the shape of a revenue, in every seven years, more than the Government price of the land; and, upon this principle, the Government would, in fact, be realizing two hundred and ten dollars every subsequent term of seven years. The whole number of acres of public land belonging to the United States at this time, or up to the 30th of September, 1848, is one billion four hundred and forty-two millions two hundred and sixteen thousand one hundred and sixty-eight acres. This amount, estimated at $1.25 per acre, will make $1,802,770,000. To dispose of $3,000,000 worth per annum, which is more than an average sum, would require seven hundred years, or a fraction less, to dispose of the entire domain. It will now be perceived at once that the Government would derive an immense advantage by giving the land to the cultivator, instead of keeping it on hand this length of time. We find by this process the Government would derive from each quarter-section in six hundred years (throwing off the large excess of nearly one hundred years), $17,000—seven going into six hundred eighty-five times. This, then, shows on the one hand what the Government would gain by giving the land away.

* * * * *

"'He said that this *exposé* ought to satisfy every one, that instead of violating the plighted faith of the Government, it was enlarging and making more valuable, and enabling the Government to derive a much larger amount of revenue to meet all its liabilities, and thereby preserving its faith inviolate.'

"I do not think there can be any question as to the revenue part of this proposition. We show that by granting a million quarter-sections you derive more revenue upon the public lands than you do by your entire land-system, as it now stands. In 1850, it was estimated that each head of a family consumed $100 worth of home manufactures. If we increase the ability of the cultivator and occupier of the soil fifty-six dollars in the family, of course it is reasonable to presume that he would consume a correspondingly increased proportion of home manufactures. Can that proposition be controverted? I think not. Then we see on the one hand, that we should derive more revenue from granting the land, on the principle laid down in the bill, and also that we should open a market for articles manufactured in our own country. Then, taking both views of the subject, we see that it is an advantage to the manufacturing interest, and that it is also an advantage to the Government, so far as imports are concerned. I should like to know, then, where can the objection be, upon the score of revenue.

"But, Mr. President, the question of dollars and cents is of no consideration to me. The money view of this subject does not influence my mind by the weight of a feather. I think it is clear, though ; and this view has been presented to prove to senators that this bill will not diminish, but, on the contrary, will increase the revenue.

"But this is not the most important view of the subject. When you look at our country as it is, you see that it is very desirable that the great mass of the people should be interested in the country. By this bill you provide a man with a home, you increase the revenue, you increase the consumption of home manufactures, and you make him a better man, and you give him an interest in the country. His condition is better. There is no man so reliable as he who is interested in the welfare of his country ; and who are more interested in the welfare of their country than those who have homes ? When a man has a home, he has a deeper, a more abiding interest in the country, and he is more reliable in all things that pertain to the Government. He is more reliable when he goes to the ballot-box ; he is more reliable in sustaining in every way the stability of our free institutions.

"It seems to me that this, without the other consideration, would be a sufficient inducement. When we see the population that is accumulating about some of our cities, I think it behooves every man who is a statesman, a patriot, and a philanthropist, to turn his attention to this subject. I have lately seen some statistics with reference to the city of New York, in which it is assumed that one-sixth of the population are paupers; that two-sixths of the population are barely able to sustain themselves; leaving one pauper to be sustained by three persons in every six in the city of New York. Does not that present a frightful state of things? Suppose the population of that city to be one million: you would have in the single city of New York one hundred and sixty-six thousand paupers.

"I do not look upon the growth of cities and the accumulation of population about cities as being the most desirable objects in this country. I do not believe that a large portion of this population, even if you were to offer them homesteads, would ever go to them. I have no idea that they would; for a man who has spent most of his life about a city, and has sunk into a pauperized condition, is not the man to go West, reclaim one hundred and sixty acres of land, and reduce it to cultivation. He will not go there on that condition. Though we are satisfied of this, may not our policy be such as to prevent, as far as practicable, the further accumulation of such an unproductive population about our cities? Let us try to prevent their future accumulation; let these live, have their day, and pass away—they will ultimately pass away—but let our policy be such as to induce men to become mechanics and agriculturists. Interest them in the country, pin them to the soil, and they become more reliable and sustain themselves, and you do away with much of the pauperism in the country. The population of the United States being twenty-eight millions, if the same proportion of paupers as in the city of New York existed throughout the country, you would have four million six hundred and sixty-six thousand paupers in the United States. Do we want all our population to become of that character?

Do we want cities to take control of this Government? Unless the proper steps be taken, unless the proper direction be given to the future affairs of this Government, the cities are to take charge of it and control it. The rural population, the mechanical and agricultural portions of this community, are the very salt of it. They constitute the "mud-sills," to use a term recently introduced here. They constitute the foundation upon which the Government rests; and hence we see the state of things before us. Should we not give the settlement of our public lands and the population of our country that direction which will beget and create the best portion of the population? Is it not fearful to think of four million six hundred and sixty-six thousand paupers in the United States, at the rate they have them in New York? Mr. Jefferson never said a truer thing than when he declared that large cities were eye-sores in the body politic: in democracies they are consuming cancers.

"I know the idea of some is to build up great populous cities, and that thereby the interests of the country are to be promoted. Sir, a city not only sinks into pauperism, but into vice and immorality of every description that can be enumerated; and I would not vote for any policy that I believed would build up cities upon this principle. Build up your villages, build up your rural districts, and you will have men who rely upon their own industry, who rely upon their own efforts, who rely upon their own ingenuity, who rely upon their own economy and application to business for a support; and these are the people whom you have to depend upon. Why, Mr. President, how was it in ancient Rome? I know there has been a great deal said in denunciation of agrarianism and the Gracchi. It has been said that a doctrine something like this led to the decline of the Roman empire ; but the Gracchi never had their day until a cancerous influence had destroyed the very vitals of Rome ; and it was the destruction of Rome that brought forth Tiberius Gracchus. It was to prevent land monopoly, not agrarianism, in the common acceptation of the term—which is dividing out lands that had been acquired by individuals. They sought to take back and put in the possession of the great mass of the people that portion of the public domain which had been assumed by the capitalists, who had no title to it in fact. The Gracchi tried to carry out this policy—to restore that which had been taken from the people. The population had sunk into the condition of large proprietors on the one hand, and dependents on the other ; and when this dependent condition was brought about, as we find from Niebuhr's History, the middle class of the community was all gone ; it had left the country ; there was nothing but an aristocracy on the one hand, and dependents upon that aristocracy on the other ; and when this got to be the case, the Roman empire went down.

"Having this illustrious example before us, we should be warned by it. Our true policy is to build up the middle class, to sustain the villages, to populate the rural districts, and let the power of this Government remain with the middle class. I want no miserable city rabble on the one hand ; I want no pampered, bloated, corrupted aristocracy on the other. I want the middle portion of society to be built up and sustained, and to let them have the control of the Government. I am as much opposed to agrarianism as any senator on this floor, or any individual in the United States. And this bill does not partake in the slightest degree of agrarianism ; but, on the contrary, it commences with men at the precise point where agrarianism ends, and it carries them up in an ascending line, while that carries them down. It gives them an interest in their country, an interest in public affairs ; and when you are involved in war, in insurrection, or rebellion, or danger of any kind, they are the men who are to sustain you. If you should have occasion to call volunteers into the service of the country, you will have a population of men having homes, having wives and children to care for, who will defend their hearthstones when invaded. What a sacred thing it is to a man to feel that he has a hearthstone to defend, a home, and a wife and children to care for, and to rest satisfied that they have an abiding-place! Such a man is interested individually in repelling invasion; he is interested individually in having good government.

"I know there are many, and even some in the Democratic ranks, whose nerves are a little timid in regard to trusting the people with too much power. Sir, the people are the safest, the best, and the most reliable lodgment of power, if you have a population of this kind. Keep up the middle class ; lop off an aristocracy on the one hand, and a rabble on the other ; let the middle class maintain the ascendency, let them have the power, and your Government is always secure. Then you need not fear the people. I know, as I have just remarked, that some are timid in regard to trusting the people ; but there can be no danger from a people who are interested in their Government, who have homes to defend, and wives and children to care for. Even if we test this proposition by that idea of self-interest which is said to govern and control man, I ask you if a man who has an interest in his country is not more reliable than one who has none ? Is not a man who is adding to the wealth of his country more reliable than one who is simply a consumer and has no interest in it ? If we suppose a man to be governed only by the principle of self-interest, is he not more reliable when he has a stake in the country, and is it not his interest to promote and advance his own condition ? Is it not the interest of the great mass to have every thing done rightly in reference to Government ? The great mass of the people hold no office ; they expect nothing from the Government. The only way they feel, and know, and understand the operations of the Government is in the exactions it makes from them. When they are receiving from the Government protection in common, it is their interest to do right in all governmental affairs ; and that being their interest, they are to be relied upon, even if you suppose men to be actuated altogether by the principle of self-interest. It is the interest of the middle class to do right in all governmental affairs ; and hence they are to be relied upon. Instead of requiring you to keep up your armies, your mounted men, and your footmen on the frontier, if you will let the people go and possess this public land on the conditions proposed in this bill, you will have an army on the frontier composed of men who will defend their own firesides, who will take care of their own homes, and will defend the other portions of the country, if need be, in time of war.

"I would remark in this connection, that the public lands have paid for themselves. According to the report of Mr. Stuart of Virginia, the Secretary of the Interior in 1850, it was shown that then the public lands had paid for themselves, and sixty millions over. We have received into the treasury since that time about thirty-two million dollars from the public lands. They have, therefore, already paid the Government more than they cost, and there can be no objection to this bill on the ground that the public lands have been bought with the common treasure of the whole country. Besides, this bill provides that each individual making an entry shall pay all the expenses attending it.

"We see, then, Mr. President, the effect this policy is to have on population. Let me ask here—looking to our popular elections, looking to the proper lodgment of power—is it not time that we had adopted a policy which would give us men interested in the affairs of the country, to control and sway our elections? It seems to me that this cannot long be debated; the point is too clear. The agricultural and mechanical portion of the community are to be relied upon for the preservation and continuance of this Government. The great mass of the people, the great middle class, are honest. They toil for their support, accepting no favor from Government. They live by labor. They do not live by consumption, but by production; and we should consume as small a portion of their production as it is possible for us to consume, leaving the producer to appropriate to his own use and benefit as much of the product of his own labor as it is possible in the nature of things to do. The great mass of the people need advocates—men who are honest and capable, who are willing to defend them. How much legislation is done for classes, and how little care seems to be exercised for the great mass of the people! When we are among our constituents, it is very easy to make appeals to the people and professions of patriotism; and then—I do not mean to be personal or invidious—it is very easy, when we are removed from them a short distance, to forget the people and legislate for classes, neglecting the interest of the great mass. The mechanics and agriculturists are honest, industrious, and economical. Let it not be supposed that I am against learning or education, but I might speak of the man in the rural districts in the language of Pope—

'Unlearned, he knew no schoolman's subtle art,
No language, but the language of the heart;
By nature honest, by experience wise;
Healthy by temperance and exercise.'

"This is the kind of men whom we must rely upon. Let your public lands be settled; let them be filled up; let honest men become cultivators and tillers of the soil. I do not claim to be prophetic, but I have sometimes thought that if we would properly direct our legislation in reference to our public policy, the time would come when this would be the greatest government on the face of the earth. Go to the great valley of the Mississippi; take the western slope of the mountains to the Pacific Ocean; take the whole area of this country, and we find that we have over three million square miles. Throw off one-fourth as unfit for cultivation, reducing the area of the United States to fifteen hundred million acres, and by appropriating three acres to a person, it will sustain a population of over five hundred million people; and I have no doubt, if this continent was strained to its utmost capacity, it could sustain the entire population of the world. Let us go on and carry out our destiny; interest men in the soil; let your vacant land be divided equally, so that men can have homes; let them live by their own industry; and the time will come when this will be the greatest nation on the face of the earth. Let agriculture and the mechanic arts maintain the ascendency, and other professions and pursuits be subordinate to them, for on these two all others rest.

"Since the crucifixion of our Saviour, emigration has been westward; and the poetic idea might have started long before it did—

'Westward the star of empire takes its way.'

It has been taking its way westward. The United States are filling up. We are going on to the Pacific coast. Let me raise the inquiry here, when, in the history of mankind, in the progress of nations, was there any nation that ever reached the point we now occupy? When was there a nation, in its progress, in its settlement, in its advance in all that constitutes and makes a nation great, that occupied the position we now occupy? When was there any nation that could look to the East and behold the tide of emigration coming, and, at the same time, turn around and look to the mighty West, and behold the tide of emigration approaching from that direction. The waves of emigration have usually been running in one direction, but we find the tide of emigration now changed, and we are occupying a central position on the globe. Emigration is coming to us from the East and from the West; and when our vacant territory shall be filled up, when it shall reach a population of one hundred and fifty or five hundred millions, who can say what will be our destiny?

"When our railroad system shall progress on proper principles, extending from one extreme of the country to the other, like so many arteries; when our telegraphic wires shall be stretched along them as the nerves in the human frame, and they shall run in parallel lines, and be crossed at right angles, until the whole globe, as it were, and especially this great centre, shall be covered like a network with these arteries and nerves; when the face of the globe shall flash with intelligence like the face of man; we, occupying this important point, may find our institutions so perfected, science so advanced, that instead of receiving nations from abroad, this will be the great sensorium from which our notions of religion, our notions of government, our improvements in works of every description shall radiate as from a common centre, and revolutionize the world.

"Who dares say that this is not our destiny, if we will only permit it to be fulfilled? Then let us go on with this great work of interesting men in becoming connected with the soil; interesting them in remaining in your mechanic shops; prevent their accumulation in the streets of your cities; and in doing this you will dispense with the necessity for all your pauper system. By doing this, you enable each community to take care of its own poor. By doing this, you destroy and break down the great propensity that exists with men to hang, and loiter, and perish about the cities of the Union, as is done now in the older countries.

"It is well enough, Mr. President, to see where our public lands have been going. There seems to be a great scruple now in reference to the appropriation of lands for the benefit of the people; but the Federal Government has been very liberal heretofore in granting lands to the States for railroad purposes. We can pass law after law, making grant after grant of the public lands to corporations, without alarming any one here. We have already granted to railroad monopolies, to corporations, twenty-four million two hundred and forty-seven thousand acres. Those grants hardly meet with opposition in Congress; but it seems to be very wrong, in the estimation of some, to grant lands to the people on the conditions proposed in the bill before us. We find, furthermore, that there have been granted to the States, as swamp-lands—and some of these lands will turn out to be the most productive on the globe—forty million one hundred and thirty-three thousand five hundred and sixty-five acres.

"In relation to the public lands, and the grants which have been made by the Government, I have obtained from the Commissioner of the General Land-Office several tables, which I now submit.

Estimate of the Quantities of Land which will inure to the States under Grants for Railroads, up to June 30, 1857

States.	Acres.	Date of Law.
Illinois	2,595,053	September 20, 1850.
Missouri	1,815,435	June 10, 1852; Feb. 9, 1853.
Arkansas	1,465,297	February 9, 1853.
Michigan	3,096,000	June 3, 1856.
Wisconsin	1,622,800	June 3, 1856.
Iowa	3,456,000	May 15, 1856.
Louisiana	1,102,560	June 3 and Aug. 11, 1856.
Mississippi	950,400	August 11, 1856.
Alabama	1,913,390	May 17, June 3, and Aug. 11, 1856; March 3, 1857.
Florida	1,814,400	May 17, 1856.
Minnesota	4,416,000	March 3, 1857.
Total	24,247,335	

Statement showing the Quantity of Swamp-land approved to the several States, up to 30th June, 1857.

States.	Acres.
Ohio	25,650.71
Indiana	1,250,937.51
Illinois	1,369,140.72
Missouri	3,615,966.57
Alabama	2,595.51
Mississippi	2,834,796.11
Louisiana	7,601,535.46
Michigan	5,465,232.41
Arkansas	5,920.024.94
Florida	10,396,982.47
Wisconsin	1,650,712.10
Total	40,133,564.51

Estimate of unsold and unappropriated Lands in each of the States and Territories, including surveyed and unsurveyed, offered and unoffered Lands, on the 30th June, 1856.

States and Territories.	Acres.	Number of Quarter-sections.
Ohio	43,553.34	272
Indiana	36,307.41	227
Illinois	511,662.85	3,198
Missouri	13,365,319.81	83,533
Alabama	9,459,367.74	59,121
Mississippi	5,519,390.69	34,496
Louisiana	5,933,373.83	37,083
Michigan	10,056,298.06	62,852
Arkansas	15,609,542.84	97,560
Florida	18,067,072.75	112,919
Iowa	6,237,661.03	38,985
Wisconsin	15,222,549.50	95,141
California	113,682,436.00	710,515
Minnesota Territory	82,502,608.33	515,641
Oregon "	118,913,241.31	743,208
Washington "	76,444,055.25	477,775
New Mexico "	155,210,804.00	970,067
Utah "	134,243,733.00	839,023
Nebraska "	206,984,747.00	1,293,655
Kansas "	76,361,058.00	477,256
Indian "	42,892,800.00	268,080
Total	1,107,297,572.74	6,920,607

"The table giving the estimated quantity of all our public lands, shows the feasibility of the plan in favor of which I have been speaking. I know that some gentlemen from the Southern States object to this bill because they fear that it will carry emigrants from the free States into those States. Well, sir, on this point I have drawn some conclusions from figures, which I will present to the Senate. In the State of Alabama there are now undisposed of fifty-nine thousand one hundred and twenty-one quarter-sections of land. I ask my Southern friends, would it not be better if a man in the State of Alabama should select a quarter-section there, and take the two hundred dollars it would have cost him, and expend it there, even though it might be inferior land, than to compel him to pay $1.25 an acre, and emigrate from the State of Alabama to a place where he could get better land? If you compel him to pay the higher price, it becomes his interest to leave his native State; but by permitting him to take the land and expend on its improvement what he would otherwise have to pay, and what it would cost him to move, the chances are that he will remain where he is. In the State of Mississippi there are thirty-four thousand four hundred and ninety-six quarter-sections; in Louisiana, thirty-seven thousand; in Arkansas, ninety-seven thousand; in Florida, one hundred and twelve thousand. Altogether, the quarter-sections of public lands belonging to the Government amount to six million nine hundred and twenty thousand. How feasible the plan is! I have shown, too, that it would take over six hundred years to dispose of the public lands at the rate we have been disposing of them, and that if you take one million quarter-sections and have them settled and cultivated, you will obtain more revenue, and you will enhance the remaining public lands more than the value of those the Government gives.

"I live in a Southern State; and, if I know myself, I am as good a Southern man as any one who lives within the borders of the South It seems to be feared that by this bill we compel men to go on the lands. I want to compel no man to go. I want to leave each and every man to be controlled by his own inclination, by his own interest, and not to force him; but is it statesmanlike, is it philanthropic, is it Christian, to keep a man in a State, and refuse to let him go, because, if he does go, he will help to populate some other portion of the country? If a man lives in the county in which I live, and he can, by crossing the line into another county, better his condition, I say let him go. If, by crossing the boundary of my State and going into another, he can better his condition, I say let him go. If a man can go from Tennessee into Illinois, or Louisiana, or Mississippi, or Arkansas, or any other State, and better his condition, let him go. I care not where he goes, so that he locates himself in this great area of freedom, becomes attached to our institutions, and interested in the prosperity and welfare of the country. I care not where he goes, so that he is under the protection of our Stars and Stripes. I say, let him go where he can better the condition of himself, his wife, and children; let him go where he can receive the greatest remuneration for his toil and for his labor. What kind of a policy is it to say that a man shall be locked up where he was born, and shall be confined to the place of his birth?

"Take the State of North Carolina, represented by the honorable senator before me*—and I have no doubt it is his intention to represent that people to their satisfaction—would it have been proper to require the people of North Carolina, from her early

* Mr. Clingman.

settlement to the present time, to be confined within her boundaries? Would they not have looked upon it as a hard sentence? Would they not have looked upon it as oppressive and cruel? North Carolina has supplied the Western States with a large proportion of her population, for the reason that by going West they could better their condition. Who would prevent them from doing it? Who would say to the poor man in North Carolina, that has no land of his own to cultivate, that lives upon some barren angle, or some piny plain, or in some other State upon some stony ridge, that he must plough and dig the land appointed to him by his landlord, and that he is not to emigrate to any place where he can better his condition? What is his prospect? He has to live poor; he has to live hard; and, in the end, when he dies, poverty, want, is the only inheritance he can leave his children. There is no one who has a higher appreciation of North Carolina than I have; she is my native State. I found it to be my interest to emigrate, and I should have thought it cruel and hard if I had been told that I could not leave her boundary. Although North Carolina did not afford me the advantages of education, though I cannot speak in the language of the schoolmen, and call her my cherishing mother, yet, in the language of Cowper, 'with all her faults, I love her still.' She is still my mother; she is my native State; and I love her as such, and I love her people too. But what an idea is it to present, as influencing the action of a statesman, that people may not emigrate from one State to another! Sir, I say let a man go anywhere within the boundaries of the United States where he can better his condition.

"Mr. President, if I entertained the notions that some of my friends who oppose this bill do, I should be a more ardent advocate of its policy than I am now, if that were possible. My friend from Alabama* entertains some strange notions in reference to democracy and the people ; and in his speech on the fisheries bill, he gave this proposition a kind of side-blow, a lick by indirection. I do not object to that ; but if I entertained his opinions, I should be a more determined and zealous advocate of the policy of this bill than I am now, if that were possible. In his speech upon the Lecompton Constitution, that senator, in speaking of the powers of the convention which framed the Constitution, said :

"'In my opinion, they would have acted in stricter accordance with the spirit and genius of our institutions if they had not submitted it in whole or in part to the popular vote. Our governments are republics, not democracies. The people exercise their sovereignty, not in person at the ballot-box, but through agents, delegates, or representatives. Our fathers founded republican governments in preference to democracies, not so much because it would be impracticable as because it would be unwise and inexpedient for the people themselves to assemble and adopt laws.'

"I have always thought the general idea had been that it was not practicable to do every thing in a strict democratic sense, and that it was more convenient for the people to appear through their delegates. But the senator said further :

* Mr. Clay.

"'They were satisfied, from reading and reflection, of the truth of Mr. Madison's observation about pure democracies, that they "have ever been spectacles of turbulence and contention; have ever been found incompatible with personal security, or the rights of property; and have, in general, been as short in their lives as they have been violent in their deaths."

* * * * * *

"'They knew that a large body of men is more liable to be controlled by passion or by interest than a single individual, and is more apt to sacrifice the rights of the minority, because it can be done with more impunity. Hence they endeavored to impose restraints upon themselves. Hence they committed the making of all their laws, organic or municipal, to their delegates or representatives, whose crimes they could punish, whose errors they could correct, and whose powers they could reclaim.

"'The great security of our rights of life, liberty, and property is in the responsibility of those who make and of those who execute the law. Establish as a principle that, to give sanction to law, it must be approved by a majority at the ballot-box, and you take away this security and surrender those rights to the most capricious, rapacious, and cruel of tyrants. I regret to see the growing spirit in Congress and throughout the country to democratize our Government; to submit every question, whether pertaining to organic or municipal laws, to the vote of the people. This is sheer radicalism; it is the Red Republicanism of revolutionary France, which appealed to the sections on all occasions, and not the American Republicanism of our fathers. Their republicanism was stable and conservative ; this is mutable and revolutionary. Theirs afforded a shield for the minority; this gives a sword to the majority. Theirs defended the rights of the weak ; this surrenders them to the power of the strong. God forbid that the demagogism of this day should prevail over the philanthropic and philosophic statesmanship of our fathers.'

"In the same speech the senator said :

"'Property is the foundation of every social fabric. To preserve, protect, and perpetuate rights of property, society is formed and government is framed.'

"Now, if I entertained these notions, I should unquestionably go for the homestead bill. I am free to say, here, that I do not hold the doctrine advanced by the honorable gentleman from Alabama to the extent that he goes. I believe the people are capable of self-government. I think they have demonstrated it most clearly ; and I do not think the senator's history of democracy states the case as it should be. I presume in the senator's own State the people acted directly upon their Constitution at the ballot-box. That is the organic law. If they did not there, they have done so in most of the States of the Union ; not, perhaps, in the original formation of their governments, but as the people have gone on and advanced in popular government. The honorable senator seems to be opposed to democratizing—in other words, he is opposed to popularizing our institutions ; he is afraid to trust the control of things to the people at the ballot-box. Why, sir, the organic law which confers all the power upon your State legislatures, creates the different divisions, different departments of the State. The Government is controlled at the ballot-box, and the doctrine set forth in the Constitution of Alabama is, that the people have a right to abolish and change their form of government when they think proper. The principle is clearly recognized; and on this my honorable friend and myself differ essentially. I find a similar doctrine laid down in a pamphlet which I have here:

"'In the convention that framed the Constitution of the United States, Gouverneur Morris said, that "Property is the main object of society." Mr. King said, "Property is the primary object of society." Mr. Butler contended strenuously that "Property was the only just measurer of representation. This was the great object of government; the great cause of war; the great means of carrying it on." Mr. Madison said, that "in future times a great majority of the people will not only be without landed, but any other sort of property. These will either combine under the influence of their common situation—in which case the right of property and the public liberty will not be secure in their hands—or, what is more probable, they will become the tools of opulence and ambition." Gouverneur Morris again said, "Give the votes to the people who have no property, and they will sell them to the rich, who will be able to buy them. We should not confine our attention to the present moment. The time is not far distant when this country will abound with mechanics and manufacturers, who will receive their bread from their employers. Will such men be the secure and faithful guardians of liberty?" Madison remarks, that those who opposed the property basis of representation did so on the ground that tho number of people was a fair index to the amount of property in any district.'

"These are not notions entertained by me; but they are important as the notions of some of our public men at the early formation of our Government. I entertain no such notions. If, however, the senator from Alabama holds that property is the main object and basis of society, he, above all other men, ought to go for this bill, so as to place every man in the possession of a home and an interest in his country. The very doctrine that he lays down appeals to him trumpet-tongued, and asks him to place these men in a condition where they can be relied upon. His argument is unanswerable, if it be true, in favor of the homestead bill. It is taking men out of a dependent condition; it is preventing this Government from sinking into that condition that Rome did in her decline. I ask him now, if he entertains these opinions, as promulgated in his speech, to come up and join with us in the passage of this bill, and make every man, if possible, a property-holder, interested in his country; give him a basis to settle upon, and make him reliable at the ballot-box.

"His speech is a fine production. I heard it with interest at the time it was delivered. I hold the opposite to him. Instead of the voice of the people being the voice of a demon, I go back to the old idea, and I favor the policy of popularizing all our free institutions. We are Democrats, occupying a position here from the South; we start together, but we turn our backs upon each other very soon. His policy would take the Government further from the people. I go in a direction to popularize it, and bring it nearer to the people. There is no better illustration of this than that old maxim, which is adopted in all our ordinary transactions, that 'if you want a thing done, send somebody to do it; if you want it well done, go and do it yourself.' It applies with as great force in governmental affairs as in individual affairs; and if we can advance and make the workings and operation of our Government familiar to and understood by the people, the better for us. I say, when and wherever it is practicable, let the people transact their own business; bring them more in contact with their Government, and then you will arrest expenditure, you will arrest corruption, you will have a purer and better Government.

"I hold to the doctrine that man can be advanced; that man can be elevated; that man can be exalted in his character and condition. We are told, on high authority, that he is made in the image of his God; that he is endowed with a certain amount of divinity. And I believe man can be elevated; man can become more and more endowed with divinity; and as he does, he becomes more Godlike in his character and capable of governing himself. Let us go on elevating our people, perfecting our institutions, until democracy shall reach such a point of perfection that we can exclaim with truth that the voice of the people is the voice of God.

"As I said, I have entertained different notions from those inculcated by the honorable senator. If I entertained his notions, then I should be for the homestead. I hold in my hand a document, by which it was proclaimed in 1776—

"'We hold these truths to be self-evident: that all

men are created equal; that they are endowed by their Creator with certain inalienable rights; that among these are life, liberty, and the pursuit of happiness; that to secure these rights governments are instituted among men, deriving their just powers from the consent of the governed.'

"Is property laid down there as the great element and the great basis of society? It is only one; and Mr. Jefferson laid it down in the Declaration of Independence, that it was a self-evident truth that government was instituted—for what? To protect men in life, liberty, and the pursuit of happiness. That is what Mr. Jefferson said. And who indorsed it? The men who framed the Declaration of Independence, who did not go upon the idea that property was the only element of society. The doctrine established by those who proclaimed our independence was, that life, liberty, and the pursuit of happiness were three great ends of government, and not property exclusively. When the declaration came forth from the old Congress Hall, it came forth as a column of fire and light. It declared that the security of life and liberty, and the pursuit of happiness, were the three great ends of government. Mr. Jefferson says, in his first inaugural address, which is the greatest paper that has ever been written in this Government—and I commend it to the reading of those who say they are Democrats, by way of refreshing their memories, that they may understand what are correct democratic principles—

"'Sometimes it is said that man cannot be trusted with the government of himself. Can he, then, be trusted with the government of others? Or have we found angels in the form of kings to govern him? Let history answer this question.'

"Mr. Jefferson seems to think man can be trusted with the government of himself. In the Declaration of Independence he does not embrace property; in fact, it is not referred to. But I am willing to concede that it is one of the primary and elementary principles in government. Mr. Jefferson declares the great truth that man is to be trusted; that man is capable of governing himself, and that he has a right to govern himself. In the same inaugural address of Mr. Jefferson, we find the passage usually attributed to Washington's farewell address, which has got universal circulation—that we should pursue our own policy; that we should promote our own institutions, maintaining friendly relations with all, entangling alliances with none. Let us carry out the doctrines of the inaugural address of Mr. Jefferson; let us carry out the great principles laid down in the Declaration of Independence, which this homestead bill embraces.

"But I wish to call attention to some other authority on this subject. As contradistinguished from the views of the senator from Alabama, I present the views of a recent writer* as in accordance with my own notions of democracy:

"'The democratic party represents the great principle of progress. It is onward and outward in its movements. It has a heart for action, and motives for a world. It constitutes the principle of diffusion, and is to humanity what the centrifugal force is to the revolving orbs of a universe. What motion is to

* Lamartine.

them, democracy is to principle. It is the soul in action. It conforms to the providence of God. It has confidence in man, and an abiding reliance in his high destiny. It seeks the largest liberty, the greatest good, and the surest happiness. It aims to build up the great interests of the many, to the least detriment of the few. It remembers the past, without neglecting the present. It establishes the present, without fearing to provide for the future. It cares for the weak, while it permits no injustice to the strong. It conquers the oppressor, and prepares the subjects of tyranny for freedom. It melts the bigot's heart to meekness, and reconciles his mind to knowledge. It dispels the clouds of ignorance and superstition, and prepares the people for instruction and self-respect. It adds wisdom to legislation, and improved judgment to government. It favors enterprise that yields a reward to the many and an industry that is permanent. It is the pioneer of humanity—the conservator of nations. It fails only when it ceases to be true to itself. *Vox populi, vox Dei*, has proved to be both a proverb and a prediction.

"'It is a mistake to suppose that democracy may not be advanced under different forms of government. Its own, it should be remembered, is the highest conventional form, that which precedes the lofty independence of the individual spoken of by the Apostlo to the Hebrews, who will need government but from the law which the Lord has placed in his heart.

"'In one respect, all nations are governed upon the same principle; that is, each adopts the form which it has the understanding and the power to sustain. There is in all a greater or lesser power, and it requires no profound speculation to decide which will control. A tyrannical dictator may do more to advance the true interests of democracy, than a moderate sovereign who is scrupulously guarded by an antiquated constitution; for the tyrant adds vigor to his opponents by his deeds of oppression.

"'The frequent question as to what form of government is best, is often answered without any reference to condition or application of principles. There can be properly but one answer, and yet the application of that answer may lead to great diversity of views.

"'When it is asserted that the democratic form of government is unquestionably the best, it must be considered that the answer not only designates the form preferred, but implies a confident belief in the advanced condition of the people who are to be the subjects of it. It premises the capacity for self-control, and a corresponding degree of knowledge in regard to the rights, balances, and necessities of society. It involves a discriminating appreciation of the varied duties of the man, the citizen, and the legislator. It presupposes a reasonable knowledge of the legitimate means and ends of government, enlarged views of humanity, and of the elements of national existence.

"'The democratic form of government is the best, because its standard of moral requisition is the highest. It claims for man a universality of interest, liberty, and justice. It is Christianity with its mountain beacons and guides. It is the standard of Deity based on the eternal principles of truth, passing through and rising above the yielding clouds of ignorance, into the regions of infinite wisdom. As we live on, this "pillar of cloud by day, and the pillar of fire by night," will not be taken from before the people, but stand immovable, immeasurable, and in the brightness of its glory continue to shed increasing light on a world and a universe.

"'The great objects of knowledge and moral culture of the people are among its most prominent provisions. Practical religion and religious freedom are the sunshine of its growth and glory. It is the sublime and mighty standard spoken of by the Psalmist, who exclaims, in the beautiful language of poetical conception—

"'The Lord is high above all nations, and his glory above the heavens. Who is like unto the Lord our God, who dwelleth on high; who humbleth himself to behold the things that are in heaven and in the earth? He raiseth up the poor out of the dust, and lifteth the needy out of the dunghill, that he may set him with princes, even with the princes of the people.

"'Democracy is a permanent element of progress, and is present everywhere, whatever may be the temporary form of the ruling power. Its inextinguishable fires first burst forth in an empire, and its welcome lights cheer the dark domains of despotism. While tyrants hate the patriot and exile him from their contracted dominions, the spirit of democracy invests him as a missionary of humanity, and inspires him with an eloquence which moves a world. Its lightning rays cannot be hidden; its presence cannot be banished. Dictators, kings, and emperors, are but its servants; and, as man becomes elevated to the dignity of self-knowledge and control, their administration ceases. Their rule indicates an imperfect state of society, and may be regarded as the moral props of the builder, necessary only to sustain a people in their different periods of growth. One cannot speak of them lightly, nor indulge in language that should seem to deny their fitness as the instruments of good in the hands of Providence. Their true position may be best gathered from the prediction which is based upon a knowledge of the past and present condition of man—that all kingdoms and empires must cease whenever a people have a knowledge of their rights, and acquire the power of a practical application of principles. This is the work of time. It is the work of constant, repeated trial. The child that attempts to step a hundred times and falls ; the new-fledged bird that tries its feeble wings again and again before it is able to sweep the circle of the sky with its kindred flocks, indicate the simple law upon which all strength depends, whether it be the strength of an insect, or the strength of a nation.

"'Because a people do not succeed in changing their form of government, even after repeated trials, we are not to infer that they are indulging in impracticable experiments, nor that they will be disappointed in ultimately realizing the great object of their ambition. Indeed, all failures of this class are indicative of progressive endeavor. They imply an increasing knowledge of the true dignity of man, and a growing disposition to engage in new and more and more difficult endeavors. These endeavors are but the exercise of a nation, and without them no people can ever command the elements of national existence and self-control. But inquiries in regard to so extensive a subject should be shaped within more practical limits. . . . . . .

"'The triumphs of democracy constitute the waymarks of the world. They demand no extraneous element of endurance for permanency, no fictitious splendor for embellishment, no borrowed greatness for glory. Originating in the inexhaustible sources of power, moved by the spirit of love and liberty, and guided by the wisdom which comes from the instincts and experience of the immortal soul, as developed in the people, democracy exists in the imperishable principle of progress, and registers its achievements in the institutions of freedom, and in the blessings which characterize and beautify the realities of life. Its genius is to assert and advance the true dignity of mind, to elevate the motives and affections of man, and to extend, establish, protect, and equalize the common rights of humanity.

"'Condorcet, although an aristocrat by genius and by birth, became a Democrat from philosophy.'

"A few years since a Whig member of the United States Senate sneeringly asked Senator Allen, of Ohio, the question, 'What is democracy?' The following was the prompt reply:

"'Democracy is a sentiment not to be appalled, corrupted, or compromised. It knows no baseness; it cowers to no danger; it oppresses no weakness; destructive only of despotism, it is the sole conservator of liberty, labor, and property. It is the sentiment of freedom, of equal rights, of equal obligations —the law of nature pervading the law of the land.'

"'What, sir,' asked Patrick Henry, in the Virginia Convention of 1778, 'is the genius of democracy? Let me read that clause of the Bill of Rights of Virginia which relates to this (third clause): That government is or ought to be instituted for the common benefit, protection, and security of the people, nation, or community: of all the various modes and forms of government, that is best which is capable of producing the greatest degree of happiness and safety, and is most effectually secured against the dangers of mal-administration; and that when any government shall be found inadequate or contrary to those principles, or contrary to those purposes, a majority of the community hath an indubitable, inalienable, and indefeasible right to reform, alter, or abolish it, in such manner as shall be judged the most conducive to the public weal.'*

"In the same convention Judge Marshall said—

"'What are the favorite maxims of democracy? A strict observance of justice and public faith, and a steady adherence to virtue;—these, sir, are the principles of a good government.'†

"'Democracy,' says the late Mr. Legaré, of South Carolina, in an article published in the New York Review, 'in the high and only true sense of that much-abused word, is the destiny of nations, because it is the spirit of Christianity.'‡

"I have referred to the remarks of the senator from Alabama to show that, if his doctrines were true, he should go for the passage of the homestead bill, because, in order to sustain the Government on the principles laid down by him, every man should be a property-holder. I want it understood that I enter a disclaimer to the doctrine presented by him, and merely

* Elliot's Debates, vol. iii., p. 77. † Ibid., p. 223.
‡ Ibid., vol. v., p. 297.

present his argument to show why he, above all others, ought to go for the homestead policy. I refer to Mr. Legaré, Judge Marshall, and the author of the 'History of Democracy,' as laying down my notions of democracy, as contradistinguished from those laid down by the distinguished senator from Alabama. We are both members from the Democratic party. I claim to be a Democrat, East, West, North, or South, or anywhere else. I have nothing to disguise. I have referred to the Declaration of Independence, and to Mr. Jefferson's inaugural address, for the purpose of showing that democracy means something very different from what was laid down by the distinguished senator from Alabama. I furthermore refer to these important documents to show that property is not the leading element of government and society. Mr. Jefferson lays down, as truths to be self-evident, that life, liberty, and the pursuit of happiness are the leading essentials of government.

"But it is not my purpose to dwell longer on that; and I wish to pass to the speech of the senator from South Carolina.* I disagree in much that was said by that distinguished senator; and I wish to show that he ought to go for the homestead policy, so as to interest every man in the country. If property is the leading and principal element on which society rests; if property is the main object for which government was created, the gentlemen who are the foremost, the most zealous, and most distinguished advocates of that doctrine should sustain the homestead policy. The honorable senator from South Carolina, in his

* Mr. Hammond.

speech on the Lecompton Constitution, by inuendo or indirection, had a hit at the homestead—a side-blow. He said:

"'Your people are awaking. They are coming here. They are thundering at our doors for homesteads, one hundred and sixty acres of land for nothing; and Southern senators are supporting them. Nay, they are assembling, as I have said, with arms in their hands, and demanding work at $1,000 a year for six hours a day. Have you heard that the ghosts of Mendoza and Torquemada are stalking in the streets of your great cities? That the Inquisition is at hand?'

"If this be true, as assumed by the distinguished senator from South Carolina, is it not an argument why men should be placed in a condition where they will not clamor, where they will not raise mobs to threaten Government, and demand homesteads? Interest these men in the country; give them homes, or let them take homes; let them become producers; let them become better citizens; let them be more reliable at the ballot-box. I want to take them on their ground, their principle, that property is the main element of society and of government; and if their doctrine be true, the argument is still stronger in favor of the homestead than the position I assume. But the distinguished senator from South Carolina goes on:

"'In all social systems there must be a class to do the menial duties, to perform the drudgery of life. That is, a class requiring but a low order of intellect, and but little skill. Its requisites are vigor, docility, fidelity. Such a class you must have, or you would not have that other class which leads progress, civilization, and refinement. It constitutes the very mudsill of society and of political government; and you might as well attempt to build a house in the air, as to build either the one or the other except on this mudsill.

" 'The poor ye always have with you; for the man who lives by daily labor, and scarcely lives at that, and who has to put out his labor in the market, and take the best he can get for it—in short, your whole hireling class of manual laborers and "operatives," as you call them, are essentially slaves. The difference between us is, that our slaves are hired for life and well compensated; there is no starvation, no begging, no want of employment among our people; and not too much employment either. Yours are hired by the day, not cared for, and scantily compensated, which may be proved in the most painful manner, at any hour, in any street in any of your large towns. Why, you meet more beggars in one day, in any single street of the city of New York, than you would meet in a lifetime in the whole South. We do not think that whites should be slaves either by law or necessity.'

"In this portion of the senator's remarks I concur. I do not think whites should be slaves; and if slavery is to exist in this country, I prefer black slavery to white slavery. But what I want to get at is, to show that my worthy friend from South Carolina should defend the homestead policy, and the impolicy of making the invidious remarks that have been made here in reference to a portion of the population of the United States. Mr. President, so far as I am concerned, I feel that I can afford to speak what are my sentiments. I am no aspirant for any thing on the face of God Almighty's earth. I have reached the summit of my ambition. The acme of all my hopes has been attained, and I would not give the position I occupy here to-day for any other in the United States. Hence, I say, I can afford to speak what I believe to be true.

"In one sense of the term, we are all slaves. A man is a slave to his ambition; he is a slave to his avarice; he is a slave to his necessities; and, in enumerations of this kind, you can scarcely find any man, high or low in society, but who, in some sense, is a slave; but they are not slaves in the sense we mean at the South, and it will not do to assume that every man who toils for his living is a slave. If that be so, all are slaves; for all must toil more or less, mentally or physically. But in the other sense of the term, we are not slaves. Will it do to assume that the man who labors with his hands, every man who is an operative in a manufacturing establishment or a shop, is a slave? No, sir; that will not do. Will it do to assume that every man who does not own slaves, but has to live by his own labor, is a slave? That will not do. If this were true, it would be very unfortunate for a good many of us, and especially so for me. I am a laborer with my hands, and I never considered myself a slave, in the acceptation of the term slave in the South. I do own some; I acquired them by my industry, by the labor of my hands. In that sense of the term I should have been a slave while I was earning them with the labor of my hands."

"Mr. Hammond. Will the senator define a slave?

"Mr. Johnson. What we understand to be a slave

in the South is a person who is held to service during his or her natural life, subject to, and under the control of, a master who has the right to appropriate the products of his or her labor to his own use. The necessities of life, and the various positions in which a man may be placed, operated upon by avarice, gain, or ambition, may cause him to labor; but that does not make a slave. How many men are there in society who go out and work with their own hands, who reap in the field and mow in a meadow, who hoe corn, who work in the shops! Are they slaves? If we were to go back and follow out this idea, that every operative and laborer is a slave, we should find that we have had a great many distinguished slaves since the world commenced. Socrates, who first conceived the idea of the immortality of the soul, pagan as he was, labored with his own hands; yes, wielded the chisel and the mallet, giving polish and finish to the stone; he afterwards turned to be a fashioner and constructor of the mind. Paul, the great expounder, himself was a tent-maker, and worked with his hands: was he a slave? Archimedes, who declared that, if he had a place on which to rest the fulcrum, with the power of his lever he could move the world: was he a slave? Adam, our great father and head, the lord of the world, was a tailor by trade: I wonder if he was a slave?

"When we talk about laborers and operatives, look at the columns that adorn this chamber, and see their finish and style. We are lost in admiration at the architecture of your buildings, and their massive columns. We can speak with admiration. What would it have been but for hands to construct it? Was the artisan who worked upon it a slave? Let us go to the South and see how the matter stands there. Is every man that is not a slaveholder to be denominated a slave because he labors? Why indulge in such a notion? The argument cuts at both ends of the line, and this kind of doctrine does us infinite harm in the South. There are operatives there; there are laborers there; there are mechanics there. Are they slaves? Who is it in the South that gives us title and security to the institution of slavery? Who is it, let me ask every Southerner around me? Suppose, for instance, we take the State of South Carolina—and there are many things about her and her people that I admire—we find that the 384,984 slaves in South Carolina are owned by how many whites? They are owned by 25,556. Take the State of Tennessee, with a population of 800,000—239,000 slaves are owned by 33,864 persons. The slaves in the State of Alabama are owned by 29,295 whites. The whole number of slaveholders in all the Slave States, when summed up, makes 347,000, owning three and a half million slaves. The white population in South Carolina is 274,000; the slaves greater than the whites. The aggregate population of the State is 668,507.

"The operatives in South Carolina are 68,549. Now, take the 25,000 slave-owners out, and a large proportion of the people of South Carolina work with their hands. Will it do to assume that, in the State of South Carolina, the State of Tennessee, the State of Alabama, and the other slaveholding States, all those who do not own slaves are slaves themselves? Will this assumption do? What does it do at home in our own States? It has a tendency to raise prejudice, to engender opposition to the institution of slavery itself. Yet our own folks will do it."

Mr. Mason: "Will the senator from Tennessee allow me to interrupt him for a moment?"

Mr. Johnson: "Yes, sir."

Mr. Mason: "The senator is making an exhibition of the very few slaveholders in the Southern States, in proportion to the white population, according to the census. That is an exhibition which has been made before by senators who sit on the other side of the Chamber. They have brought before the American people what they allege to be the fact, shown by the census, that of the white population in the Southern States, there are very few who are slaveholders. The senator from Tennessee is now doing the same thing. I understand him to say there are but some—I do not remember exactly the number, but I think three thousand, or a fraction more—of the whites in the slaveholding States, who own three million slaves; but he made no further exposition. I ask the senator to state the additional fact, that the holders of the slaves are the heads of families of the white population; and neither that senator nor those whose example he has followed on the other side, has stated the fact that the white population in the Southern States, as in the other States, embraces men, women, and children. He has exhibited only the number of slaveholders who are heads of families."

Mr. Johnson: "The senator says I have not made an exhibit of the fact. The senator interrupted me before I had concluded. I gave way as a matter of courtesy to him. Perhaps his speech would have had no place, if he had waited to hear me a few moments longer."

Mr. Mason: "I shall wait. I thought the senator had passed that point."

Mr. Johnson: "I was stating the fact, that according to the census tables three hundred and forty-seven thousand white persons owned the whole number of slaves in the Southern States. I was about to state that the families holding these slaves might average six or eight or ten persons, all of whom are interested in the products of slave-labor, and many of these slaves are held by minors and by females. I was not alluding to the matter for the purpose the senator from Virginia seems to have intimated, and should have been much obliged to him if he had waited until he heard my application of these figures. I was going to show that expressions like those to which I have alluded operate against us in the South, and I was following the example of no one. I was taking these facts from the census tables, which were published by order of Congress, to show the bad policy and injustice of declaring that the laboring portion of our population were slaves and menials. Such declarations should not be applied to the people either North or South. I wished to say in that connection, that, in my opinion, if a few men at the North and at the South, who entertain extreme views on the subject of slavery, and desire to keep up agitation, were out of the way, the great mass of the people, North and South, would go on prosperously and harmoniously under our institutions.

* * * * * *

"Sir, carry out the homestead policy, attach the people to the soil, induce them to love the Government, and you will have the North reconciled to the

South, and the South to the North, and we shall not have invidious doctrines preached to stir up bad feelings in either section. I know that in my own State, and in the other Southern States, the men who do not own slaves are among the first to take care of the institution. They will submit to no encroachment from abroad, no interference from other sections.

"I have said, Mr. President, much more than I intended to say, and, I fear, in rather a desultory manner, but I hope I have made myself understood. I heard that some gentleman was going to offer an amendment to this bill, providing that the Government should furnish every man with a slave. So far as I am concerned, if it suited him, and his inclination led him that way, I wish to God every head of a family in the United States had one to take the drudgery and menial service off his family. I would have no objection to that; but this intimation was intended as a slur upon my proposition. I want that to be determined by the people of the respective States, and not by the Congress of the United States. I do not want this body to interfere by inuendo or by amendment, prescribing that the people shall have this or the other. I desire to leave that to be determined by the people of the respective States, and not by the Congress of the United States.

"I hope, Mr. President, that this bill will be passed. I think it involves the very first principles of the Government; it is founded upon statesmanship, humanity, philanthropy, and even upon Christianity itself. I know the argument has been made, why permit one portion of the people to go and take some of this land and not another? The law is in general terms; it places it in the power of every man who will go, to take a portion of the land. The Senator from Alabama suggests to me that a person, in order to get the benefit of this bill, must prove that he is not the owner of other land. An amendment was yesterday inserted in the bill striking out that provision. Then it places all on an equality to go and take. Why should this not be done? It was conceded yesterday that the land was owned by the people. There are over three million heads of families in the United States; and if every man who is the head of a family were to take a quarter-section of public land, there would still be nearly four million quarter-sections left. If some people go and take quarter-sections, it does not interfere with the rights of others, for he who goes takes only a part of that which is his, and takes nothing that belongs to anybody else. The domain belongs to the whole people; the equity is in the great mass of the people; the Government holds the fee and passes the title, but the beneficial interest is in the people. There are, as I have said, two quarter-sections of land for every head of a family in the United States, and we merely propose to permit a head of a family to take one-half of that which belongs to him.

"I believe the passage of this bill will strengthen the bonds of the Union. It will give us a better voting population, and just in proportion as men become interested in property, they will become reconciled to all the institutions of property in the country, in whatever shape they may exist. Take the institution of slavery, for instance: would you rather trust it to the mercies of a people liable to be ruled by the mobs of which my honorable friend from South Carolina spoke, or would you prefer an honest set of landholders? Which would be the most reliable? Which would guarantee the greatest security to our institutions, when they come to the test of the ballot-box?

"Mr. President, I hope the Senate will pass this bill. I think it will be the beginning of a new state of things—a new era.

"So far as I am concerned—I say it not in any spirit of boasting or egotism—if this bill were passed, and the system it inaugurates carried out, of granting a reasonable quantity of land for a man's family, and looking far into the future I could see resulting from it a stable, an industrious, a hardy, a Christian, a philanthropic community, I should feel that the great object of my little mission was fulfilled. All that I desire is the honor and the credit of being one of the American Congress to consummate and to carry out this great scheme, that is to elevate our race and to make our institutions more permanent. I want no reputation, as some have insinuated. You may talk about Jacobinism, Red Republicanism, and so on. I pass by such insinuations as the idle wind, which I regard not.

"I know the motives that prompt me to action. I can go back to that period in my own history when I could not say that I had a home. This being so, when I cast my eyes from one extreme of the United States to the other, and behold the great number that are homeless, I feel for them. I believe this bill would put them in possession of homes; and I want to see them realizing that sweet conception when each man can proclaim, 'I have a home; an abiding-place for my wife and for my children ; I am not the tenant of another; I am my own ruler; and I will move according to my own will, and not at the dictation of another.' Yes, Mr. President, if I should never be heard of again on the surface of God's habitable globe, the proud satisfaction of having contributed my little aid to the consummation of this great measure is all the reward I desire.

" The people need friends. They have a great deal to bear. They make all ; they do all ; but how little they participate in the legislation of the country ! All, or nearly all, of our legislation is for corporations, for monopolies, for classes, and individuals; but the great mass who produce while we consume are little cared for ; their rights and interests are neglected and overlooked. Let us, as patriots, as statesmen, let us, as Christians, consummate this great measure, which will exert an influence throughout the civilized world in fulfilling our destiny. I thank the Senate for their attention."

CHAPTER III.

STATE OF THE UNION.

Two distinguishing qualities of President Johnson's mind are firmness and independence. Convinced of the correctness of his opinions, he never shrinks from their natural and logical consequences. Opposed from the very outset of his career to the doctrine of the right of a State to withdraw at pleasure from the Federal Union, when the great and eventful crisis came he was ready to meet it with dauntless courage and unfaltering faith. He broke from old ties of personal and political associations without a moment's hesitation, and threw himself into the fight. "to do or die" in defence of the national flag and an undivided country.

In a speech delivered in the Senate the 5th and 6th of February, 1861, after certain States had formally seceded and declared themselves separate and foreign communities, he seemed to rise with the occasion, and to pour forth in a stronger tide the power of his logic and the thunder-roll of his eloquence. This great effort was on the state of the Union, the Senate having under consideration the message of the President communicating resolutions of the Legislature of Virginia. Gladly would we transcribe the whole of this able speech, in the course of which the heresy he combated was cut up by the roots and thrown to the winds, but our space will only permit the insertion of its thrilling and soul-stirring conclusion:

"There is no one in the United States who is more willing to do justice to the distinguished senator from Mississippi than myself; and when I consider his early education; when I look at his gallant services, finding him first in the military school of the United States, educated by his Government, taught the science of war at the expense of his country—taught to love the principles of the Constitution; afterwards entering its service, fighting beneath the Stars and Stripes to which he has so handsomely alluded, winning laurels that are green and imperishable, and bearing upon his person scars that are honorable; some of which have been won at home; others of which have been won in a foreign clime, and upon other fields—I would be the last man to pluck a feather from his cap or a single gem from the chaplet that encircles his brow. But when I consider his early associations; when I remember that he was nurtured by this Government; that he fought for this Government; that he won honors under the flag of this Government, I cannot understand how he can be willing to hail another banner, and turn from that of his country, under which he has won laurels and received honors. This is a matter of taste, however; but it seems to me that, if I could not unsheathe my sword in vindication of the flag of my country, its glorious Stars and Stripes, I would return the sword to its scabbard ; I would never sheathe it in the bosom of my mother ; never ! never ! never !"

* * * * * * * * *

"Sir, I intend to stand by that flag, and by the Union of which it is the emblem. I agree with Mr. A. H. Stephens, of Georgia, 'that this Government of our fathers, with all its defects, comes nearer the objects of all good governments than any other on the face of the earth.'

"I have made allusions to the various senators who have attacked me, in vindication of myself. I have been attacked on all hands by some five or six, and may be attacked again. All I ask is, that, in making these attacks, they meet my positions, answer my arguments, refute my facts. I care not for the number that may have attacked me; I care not how many may come hereafter. Feeling that I am in the right, that argument, that fact, that truth are on my side, I place them all at defiance. Come one, come all ; for I feel, in the words of the great dramatic poet—

> 'Thrice is he armed that hath his quarrel just;
> And he but naked, though locked up in steel,
> Whose conscience with [treason] is corrupted.'

"I have been told, and I have heard it repeated, that this Union is gone. It has been said in this chamber, that it is in the cold sweat of death; that, in fact, it is really dead, and merely lying in state waiting for the funeral obsequies to be performed. If this be so, and the war that has been made upon me in consequence of advocating the Constitution and the Union is to result in my overthrow and in my destruction; and that flag, that glorious flag, the emblem of the Union, which was borne by Washington through a seven-years' struggle, shall be struck from the Capitol and trailed in the dust; when this Union is interred, I want no more honorable winding-sheet than that brave old flag, and no more glorious grave than to be interred in the tomb of the Union. [Applause in the galleries.] For it I have stood; for it I will continue to stand; I care not whence the blows come; and some will find, before this contest is over, that while there are blows to be given, there will be blows to receive; and that, while others can thrust, there are some who can parry. God preserve my country from the desolation that is threatening her, from treason and traitors!

> 'Is there not some chosen curse,
> Some hidden thunder in the stores of heaven,
> Red with uncommon wrath, to blast the man
> Who owes his greatness to his country's ruin?'

[Applause in the galleries.]

"In conclusion, Mr. President, I make an appeal to the conservative men of all parties. You see the posture of public affairs; you see the condition of the country; you see along the line of battle the various points of conflict; you see the struggle which the Union men have to maintain in many of the States. You ought to know and feel what is necessary to sustain those who, in their hearts, desire the preservation of this Union of States. Will you sit with stoic indifference, and see those who are willing to stand by the Constitution and uphold the pillars of the Government driven away by the raging surges that are now sweeping over some portions of the country? As conservative men, as patriots, as men who desire the preservation of this great, this good, this unparalleled Government, I ask you to save the country; or let the propositions be submitted to the people, that the heart of the nation may respond to them. I have an abiding confidence in the intelligence, the patriotism, and the integrity of the great mass of the people; and I feel in my own heart that, if this subject could be got before them, they would settle the question, and the Union of these States would be preserved." [Applause in the galleries.]

CHAPTER IV.

SPEECH ON THE WAR FOR THE UNION, DELIVERED IN THE SENATE, JULY 27, 1861.

At last came the armed collision between the Federal authority and the Confederacy of the seceding States. The latter had planted their capital at Richmond, had organized an army, and in a terrible battle, fought 21st July, 1861, had inflicted a signal defeat upon the Federal forces upon the field of Manassas. Amid the panic and discouragement that followed that disastrous day, Andrew Johnson stood steadfast as a rock, and displayed a resolution worthy of a Roman senator in the best times of the republic. Only six days after the sanguinary struggle, and while Washington itself was in danger of capture by the victorious foe, he spoke in favor of the joint resolution before the Senate to confirm and approve certain acts of President Lincoln for suppressing insurrection and rebellion. In this speech he took the ground that the present contest was the third and last trial of the country's strength. The first, he said, was in gaining her independence—the second, in defending herself against foreign invasion in the war of 1812—the third trial, he averred, was now upon us; that the nation was fighting against enemies at home—against those who have no confidence in its integrity or in the institutions that may be established under its organic law:—whether we can succeed in putting down traitors and treason, and in establishing the great fact that we have a Government, with sufficient strength to maintain its existence against whatever combination may oppose its constitutional action.

The conclusion of this noble effort is peculiarly exciting, and stirs the blood like the blast of a trumpet:

"We love the Constitution as made by our fathers. We have confidence in the integrity and capacity of the people to govern themselves. We have lived entertaining these opinions: we intend to die entertaining them. The battle has commenced. The President has placed it upon the true ground. It is an issue on the one hand for the people's Government, and its overthrow on the other. We have commenced the battle of freedom. It is freedom's cause. We are resisting usurpation and oppression. We will triumph; we must triumph. Right is with us. A great and fundamental principle of right, that lies at the foundation of all things, is with us. We may meet with impediments, and may meet with disasters, and here and there a defeat; but ultimately freedom's cause must triumph, for—

'Freedom's battle once begun,
Bequeathed from bleeding sire to son,
Though baffled oft, is ever won.'

"Yes, we must triumph. Though sometimes I cannot see my way clear, in matters of this kind as in matters of religion, when my facts give out, when my reason fails me, I draw largely upon my faith. My faith is strong, based on the eternal principles of right, that a thing so monstrously wrong as is this rebellion cannot triumph. Can we submit to it? Can bleeding justice submit to it? Is the Senate, are the American people, prepared to give up the graves of Washington and Jackson, to be encircled and governed and controlled by a combination of traitors and rebels? I say, let the battle go on—it is freedom's cause—until the Stars and Stripes (God bless them!) shall again be unfurled upon every cross-road, and from every house-top, throughout the Confederacy, north and south. Let the Union be reinstated; let the law be enforced; let the Constitution be supreme.

"If the Congress of the United States were to give up the tombs of Washington and Jackson, we should have rising up in our midst another Peter the Hermit, in a much more righteous cause—for ours is true, while his was a delusion—who would appeal to the American people, and point to the tombs of Washington and Jackson, in the possession of those who are worse than the infidel and the Turk who held the Holy Sepulchre. I believe the American people would start of their own accord, when appealed to, to redeem the graves of Washington and Jackson and Jefferson, and all the other patriots who are lying within the limits of the Southern Confederacy. I do not believe they would stop the march, until again the flag of this Union should be placed over the graves of those distinguished men. There will be an uprising. Do not talk about Republicans now; do not talk about Democrats now ; do not talk about Whigs or Americans now : talk about your country, and the Constitution, and the Union. Save that ; preserve the integrity of the Government ; once more place it erect among the nations of the earth ; and then, if we want to divide about questions that may arise in our midst, we have a Government to divide in.

"I know it has been said that the object of this war is to make war on Southern institutions. I have been in free States and I have been in slave States, and I thank God that, so far as I have been, there has been one universal disclaimer of any such purpose. It is a war upon no section ; it is a war upon no peculiar institution ; but it is a war for the integrity of the Government, for the Constitution, and the supremacy of the laws. That is what the nation understands by it.

"The people whom I represent appeal to the Government and to the nation to give us the constitutional protection that we need. I am proud to say that I have met with every manifestation of that kind in the Senate, with only a few dissenting voices. I am proud to say, too, that I believe old Kentucky (God bless her !) will ultimately rise and shake off the stupor which has been resting upon her ; and instead of denying us the privilege of passing through her borders, and taking arms and munitions of war to enable a downtrodden people to defend themselves, will not only give us that privilege, but will join us and help us in the work. The people of Kentucky love the Union ; they love the Constitution ; they have no fault to find with it; but in that State they have a duplicate to the Governor of ours. When we look all around, we see how the Governors of the different States have been involved in this conspiracy—the most stupendous and gigantic conspiracy that was ever formed, and as corrupt and as foul as that attempted by Catiline in the days of Rome. We know it to be so. Have we not known men to sit at their desks in this Chamber, using the Government's stationery to write treasonable letters; and while receiving their pay, sworn to support the Constitution and sustain the law, engaging in midnight conclaves to devise ways and means by which the Government and the Constitution should be overthrown? The charge was made and published in the papers. Many things we know that we cannot fully prove; but we know from the regular steps that were taken in this work of breaking up the Government, or trying to break it up, that there was system, concert of action. It is a scheme more corrupt than the assassination planned and conducted by Catiline in reference to the Roman Senate. The time has arrived when we should show to the nations of the earth that we are a nation capable of preserving our existence, and give them evidence that we will do it.

"I have already detained the Senate much longer than I intended when I rose, and I shall conclude in a few words more. Although the Government has met with a little reverse within a short distance of this city, no one should be discouraged and no heart should be dismayed. It ought only to prove the necessity of bringing forth, and exerting still more vigorously, the power of the Government in maintenance of the Constitution and the laws. Let the energies of the Government be redoubled, and let it go on with this war—not a war upon sections, not a war upon peculiar institutions anywhere ; but let the Constitution and the Union be inscribed on its banners, and the supremacy and enforcement of the laws be its watchword. Then it can, it will, go on triumphantly. We must succeed. This Government must not, cannot fail. Though your flag may have trailed in the dust ; though a retrograde movement may have been made ; though the banner of our country may have been sullied, let it still be borne onward ; and if, for the prosecution of this war in behalf of the Government and the Constitution, it is necessary to cleanse and purify that banner, I say let it be baptized in fire from the sun and bathed in a nation's blood ! The nation must be redeemed ; it must be triumphant. The Constitution—which is based upon principles immutable, and upon which rest the rights of man and the hopes and expectations of those who love freedom throughout the civilized world—must be maintained."

CHAPTER V.

SPEECH ON THE PROPOSED EXPULSION OF MR. BRIGHT, DELIVERED IN THE SENATE OF THE UNITED STATES, JAN. 31, 1862.

THE Senate having under consideration the following resolution, submitted by Mr. Wilkinson on the 16th of December, 1861, and which had been reported upon adversely by the Committee on the Judiciary :

"*Whereas,* Hon. Jesse D. Bright, heretofore, on the 1st day of March, 1861, wrote a letter, of which the following is a copy :

" 'MY DEAR SIR : Allow me to introduce to your acquaintance my friend, Thomas B. Lincoln, of Texas. He visits your capital mainly to dispose of what he regards a great improvement in firearms. I recommend him to your favorable consideration as a gentleman of the first respectability, and reliable in every respect.

" 'Very truly yours, JESSE D. BRIGHT.

" 'To His Excellency JEFFERSON DAVIS,

" 'President of the Confederation of States.'

"*And whereas* we believe the said letter is evidence of disloyalty to the United States, and is calculated to give aid and comfort to the public enemies; therefore,

"*Be it resolved*, That the said Jesse D. Bright is expelled from his seat in the Senate of the United States."

Mr. Johnson said:

"Mr. President, when this resolution for the expulsion of the senator from Indiana was first presented to the consideration of the Senate, it was not my intention to say a single word upon it. Presuming that action would be had upon it at a very early day, I intended to content myself with casting a silent vote. But the question has assumed such a shape that, occupying the position I do, I cannot consent to record my vote without giving some of the reasons that influence my action.

"I am no enemy of the senator from Indiana. I have no personally unkind feelings towards him. I never had any, and have none now. So far as my action on this case is concerned, it will be controlled absolutely and exclusively by public considerations, and with no reference to partisan or personal feeling. I know that since the discussion commenced, an intimation has been thrown out, which I was pained to hear, that there was a disposition on the part of some to hound down the senator from Indiana. Sir, I know that I have no disposition to 'hound' any man. I would to God that I could think it otherwise than necessary for me to say a single word upon this question, or even to cast a vote upon it. So far as I know, there has never been any unkind feeling between the senator and myself from the time we made our advent into public life down to this moment. Although party and party associations and party considerations influence all of us more or less—and I do not pretend to be free from the influence of party more than others—I know, if I know myself, that no such considerations influence me now. Not many years ago there was a contest before the Senate as to his admission as a senator from the State of Indiana; we all remember the struggle that took place. I will not say that the other side of the House were influenced by party considerations when the vote upon that question of admission took place; but if my memory serves me correctly, there was upon one side of the chamber a nearly strict party vote that he was not entitled to his seat, while on the other side his right was sustained entirely by a party vote. I was one of those who voted for the senator's admission to a seat upon this floor under the circumstances. I voted to let him into the Senate, and I am constrained to say that, before his term has expired, I am compelled to vote to expel him from it. In saying this, I repeat that if I know myself, and I think I do as well as ordinary men know themselves, I cast this vote upon public considerations entirely, and not from party or personal feeling.

"Mr. President, I hold that under the Constitution of the United States we clearly have the power to expel a member, and that, too, without our assuming the character of a judicial body. It is not necessary to have articles of impeachment preferred by the other House; it is not necessary to organize ourselves into a court for the purpose of trial; but the principle is broad and clear, inherent in the very organization of the body itself, that we have the power and the right to expel any member from the Senate whenever we deem that the public interests are unsafe in his hands, and that he is unfit to be a member of the body. We all know, and the country understands, that provision of the Constitution which confers this power upon the Senate. Judge Story, in commenting upon the case of John Smith, in connection with the provision of the Constitution to which I have referred, used the following language:

"'The precise ground of the failure of the motion does not appear; but it may be gathered, from the arguments of his counsel, that it did not turn upon any doubt that the power of the Senate extended to cases of misdemeanor not done in the presence or view of the body; but most probably it was decided upon some doubt as to the facts. It may be thought difficult to draw a clear line of distinction between the right to inflict the punishment of expulsion and any other punishment upon a member, founded on the time, place, or nature of the offence. The power to expel a member is not, in the British House of Commons, confined to offences committed by the party as a member, or during the session of Parliament; but it extends to all cases where the offence is such as, in the judgment of the House, unfits him for parliamentary duties.'*

"The rule in the House of Commons was undoubtedly in the view of the framers of our Constitution; and the question is, has the member unfitted himself,

* *Story's Commentaries on the Constitution.*

has he disqualified himself, in view of the extraordinary condition of the country, from discharging the duties of a senator? Looking at his connection with the executive; looking at the condition, and probably the destinies of the country, we are to decide—without prejudice, without passion, without excitement—can the nation, and does the nation, have confidence in committing its destinies to the senator from Indiana, and others who are situated like him?

"If we were disposed to bring to our aid, and were willing to rely upon the public judgment, what should we find? When you pass through the country, the common inquiry is, 'Why has not Senator Bright, and why have not others like him, been expelled from the Senate?' I have had the question asked me again and again. I do not intend, though, to predicate my action as a senator upon what may be simply rumor and popular clamor or popular indignation; but still it is not often the case that when there is a public judgment formed in reference to any great question before the country, that public judgment is not well founded, though it is true there are sometimes exceptions.

"Having shown our power in the premises to be clear, according to the general authority granted by the Constitution, and the broad principle stated by Judge Story in its elucidation, I next turn my attention to the case itself. The senator from Indiana is charged with having written a letter, on the 1st of March last, to the chief of the rebellion, and this is the basis of this proceeding against him. What was the condition of the country at the time that letter was written? Did war then exist, or not? for really that is the great point in the case. On that point allow me to read an extract from the charge of Judge David A. Smalley to the grand-jury of the United States District Court for the Southern District of New York, published in the 'National Intelligencer' of January 21, 1861 :

"'It is well known that war, civil war, exists in portions of the Union ; that persons owing allegiance to the United States have confederated together, and with arms, by force and intimidation, have prevented the execution of the constitutional acts of Congress, have forcibly seized upon and hold a custom-house and post-office, forts, arsenals, vessels, and other property belonging to the United States, and have actually fired upon vessels bearing the United States flag and carrying United States troops. This is a usurpation of the authority of the Federal Government ; it is high treason by levying war. Either one of those acts will constitute high treason. There can be no doubt of it.'

"The judge here defines high treason, and he goes on to say :

"'What amounts to adhering to and giving aid and comfort to our enemies, it is somewhat difficult in all cases to define ; but certain it is that furnishing them with arms,'—

"It really seems that by some kind of intuition the judge had in his mind the precise case now under our consideration, and had anticipated it last January,—

—"'certain it is that furnishing them with arms or munitions of war, vessels or other means of transportation, or any materials which will aid the traitors in carrying out their traitorous purposes, with a knowledge that they are intended for such purposes, or inciting and encouraging others to engage in or aid the traitors in any way, does come within the provisions of the act.'

"In this view, even if we were sitting as a court, bound by the rules and technicalities of judicial proceedings, should we not be bound to hold that this case comes within this legal definition?

"'And it is immaterial,' adds Judge Smalley, 'whether such acts are induced by sympathy with the rebellion, hostility to the Government, or a design for gain.'

"In view of these authorities let us look at the letter. It was written on the 1st of March, 1861. The opinion of Judge Smalley was published in the 'Intelligencer' of the 21st of January, 1861, and must, of course, have been delivered before that time. It would be doing the senator's intelligence great injustice to presume that he was not as well informed on the subject as the judge was who was charging the grand-jury in reference to an act of Congress passed at an early day in the history of the Government. It would be doing him great injustice to suppose that he was not familiar with the statute. It would be doing him great injustice to suppose that he had not observed the fact that the attention of the country was being called by the courts to the treason that was rampant throughout the land. The letter complained of is as follows:

"'WASHINGTON, March 1, 1861.

"'MY DEAR SIR—Allow me to introduce to your acquaintance my friend Thomas B. Lincoln, of Texas.

He visits your capital mainly to dispose of what he regards a great improvement in firearms. I recommend him to your favorable consideration as a gentleman of the first respectability, and reliable in every respect.

"'Very truly yours,

"'JESSE D. BRIGHT.

"'To His Excellency JEFFERSON DAVIS,
"'President of the Confederation of States.'

"According to the charge of Judge Smalley, which I have already read, the flag of the United States had been fired upon before the 21st of January, 1861, and war then did in fact exist. When the rebels were taking our forts; when they were taking possession of our post-offices; when they were seizing our custom-houses; when they were taking possession of our mints and the depositories of the public money, can it be possible that the senator from Indiana did not know that war existed, and that rebellion was going on? It is a fact that the ordinance of the convention of Texas seceding from the Union, and attaching herself to the Southern Confederacy, was dated back as far as the 1st of February, 1861. Then, at the time the letter was written, Thomas B. Lincoln was a citizen of a rebel State; a traitor and a rebel himself. He comes to the senator asking him to do what? To write a letter by which he could be facilitated in his scheme of selling an improved firearm, an implement of war and of death. Can there be any mistake about it? He asks for a letter recommending an improved firearm to the president of the rebel States, who was then in actual war; the man who asked for this being himself from a State that was in open rebellion, and he himself a traitor.

"Now, sir, if we were a court, how would the case be presented? I know the Constitution says that 'no person shall be convicted of treason unless on the testimony of two witnesses to the same overt act, or on confession in open court.' Here is an overt act; it is shown clearly and plainly. We have the Senator's confession in open Senate that he did write the letter. Shall we with this discretion, in view of the protection of this body and the safety of the Government, decide the case upon special pleas or hunt up technicalities by which the senator can escape, as you would quash an indictment in a criminal court?

"The case of John Smith has already been stated to the Senate. A true bill has been found against him for his connection with Burr's treason, but upon a technicality, the proof not being made out according to the Constitution, and Burr having been tried first and acquitted, the bill against Smith was quashed, as he was only an accomplice. He was, therefore, turned out of court; the proceedings against him were quashed upon a technicality; but John Smith was a senator, and he came here to this body. He came again to take his seat in the Senate of the United States, and what did the Senate do? They took up his case; they investigated it. Mr. Adams made a report, able, full, complete. I may say he came well-nigh exhausting the whole subject. The committee reported a resolution for his expulsion, and how did the vote stand? It is true that Mr. Smith was not expelled, for the want of some little formality in this body, the vote standing 19 to 10. It only lacked one vote to put him out by a two-thirds majority, according to the requirements of the Constitution. What was the judgment of the nation? It was that John Smith was an accomplice of Burr, and the Senate condemned him and almost expelled him, not narrowing itself down to those rules and technicalities that are resorted to in courts and by which criminals escape. To show the grounds upon which the action in that case was based, I beg leave to read some extracts from Mr. John Quincy Adams' report:

"'In examining the question whether these forms of judicial proceedings or the rules of judicial evidence ought to be applied to the exercise of that censorial authority which the Senate of the United States possesses over the conduct of its members, let us assume as the test of their application either the dictates of unfettered reason, the letter and spirit of the Constitution, or precedents domestic or foreign, and your committee believe that the result will be the same: that the power of expelling a member must in its nature be discretionary, and in its exercise always more summary than the tardy process of judicial proceedings.

"'The power of expelling a member for misconduct results, on the principles of common sense, from the interests of the nation that the high trust of legislation should be invested in pure hands. When the trust is elective, it is not to be presumed that the constituent body will commit the deposit to the keeping of worthless characters. But when a man, whom his fellow-citizens have honored with their confidence on the pledge of a spotless reputation, has degraded himself by the commission of infamous crimes, which become suddenly and unexpectedly revealed to the world, defective, indeed, would be that institution which should be impotent to discard from its bosom the contagion of such a member; which should have no remedy of amputation to apply until the poison had reached the heart.'"

* * * * * *

"'But when a member of a legislative body lies under the imputation of aggravated offences, and the determination upon his case can operate only to remove him from a station of extensive powers and important trusts, this disproportion between the interest of the public and the interest of the individual disappears; if any disproportion exists, it is of an opposite kind. It is not better that ten traitors should be members of this Senate, than that one innocent man should suffer expulsion. In either case, no doubt, the evil would be great; but in the former, it would strike at the vitals of the nation; in the latter it might, though deeply to be lamented, only be the calamity of an individual.'"

* * * * * *

"'Yet in the midst of all this anxious providence of legislative virtue, it has not authorized the constituent body to recall in any case its representative. It has not subjected him to removal by impeachment; and when the darling of the people's choice has become their deadliest foe, can it enter the imagination of a reasonable man, that the sanctuary of their legislation must remain polluted with his presence, until a court of common law, with its pace of snail, can ascertain whether his crime was committed on the right or on the left bank of a river; whether a puncture of difference can be found between the words of the charge and the words of the proof; whether the witnesses of his guilt should or should not be heard by his jury; and whether he was punishable, because present at an overt act, or intangible to public justice because he only contrived and prepared it? Is it conceivable that a traitor to that country which has loaded him with favors, guilty to the common understanding of all mankind, should be suffered to return unquestioned to that post of honor and confidence where, in the zenith of his good fame, he had been placed by the esteem of his countrymen, and in defiance of their wishes, in mockery of their fears, surrounded by the public indignation, but inaccessible to its bolt, pursue the purposes of treason in the heart of the national councils? Must the assembled rulers of the land listen with calmness and indifference, session after session, to the voice of notorious infamy, until the sluggard step of municipal justice can overtake his enormities? Must they tamely see the lives and fortunes of millions, the safety of present and future ages, depending upon his vote, recorded with theirs, merely because the abused benignity of general maxims may have remitted to him the forfeiture of his life?

"'Such, in very supposable cases, would be the unavoidable consequences of a principle which should offer the crutches of judicial tribunals as an apology for crippling the congressional power of expulsion. Far different, in the opinion of your committee, is the spirit of our Constitution. They believed that the very purpose for which this power was given was to preserve the Legislature from the first approaches of infection; that it was made discretionary, because it could not exist under the procrastination of general rules. That its process must be summary, because it would be rendered nugatory by delay.'

"Mr. President, suppose Aaron Burr had been a senator, and after his acquittal he had come back here to take his seat in the Senate, what would have been done? According to the doctrine avowed in this debate, that we must sit as a court and subject the individual to all the rules and technicalities of criminal proceedings, could he have been expelled? And yet is there a senator here who would have voted to allow Aaron Burr to take a seat in the Senate after his acquittal by a court and jury? No; there is not a senator here who would have done it. Aaron Burr was tried in court, and he was found not guilty; he was turned loose; but was the public judgment of this nation less satisfied of his guilt than if he had not been acquitted? What is the nation's judgment, settled and fixed? That Aaron Burr was guilty of treason, notwithstanding he was acquitted by a court and jury.

"It is said by some senators that the senator from Indiana wrote this letter simply as a letter of friendship. Sir, just think of it! A senator of the United States was called upon to write a letter for a rebel, for a man from a rebel State, after the courts of the country had pronounced that civil war existed; after the judicial tribunals had defined what aiding and adhering to the enemies of the country was! Under such circumstances, what would have been the course of loyalty and of patriotism? Suppose a man who had been your friend, sir, who had rendered you many acts of kindness, had come to you for such a letter. You would have asked where he was going with it. You would have said, 'There is a Southern Confederacy; there is a rebellion; my friend, you cannot ask me to write a letter to anybody there; they are at war with the United States; they are at war with my Government; I cannot write you a letter giving you aid and assistance in selling your improved firearm there.' Why? 'Because that firearm may be used against my own country and against my own fellow-citizens. Would not that have been the language of a man who was willing to recognize his obligations of duty to his country?

What was the object of writing the letter? It certainly was to aid, to facilitate the selling of his firearms, to inspire the rebel chief with confidence in the individual. It was saying substantially, 'I know this man; I write to you because I know you have confidence in me; I send him to you because I know you need firearms; you need improved firearms; you need the most deadly and destructive weapons of warfare to overcome this great and this glorious country; I recommend him to you, and I recommend his firearms; he is a man in whom entire confidence may be placed.' That, sir, is the letter. I have already shown the circumstances under which it was written. If such a letter had been written in the purest innocence of intention, with no treasonable design, with no desire to injure his own Government, yet, in view of all the circumstances, in view of the facts which had transpired, a senator who would be so unthoughtful, and so negligent, and so regardless of his country's interests as to write such a letter, is not entitled to a seat on this floor.' [Applause in the galleries.]

The presiding officer*—Order! order!

Mr. Johnson:

"Then, Mr. President, what has been the bearing and the conduct of the senator from Indiana since? I desire it to be understood that I refer to him in no unkindness, for God knows I bear him none; but my duty I will perform. 'Duties are mine, consequences are God's.' What has been the senator's bearing generally? Have you heard of his being in the field? Have you heard of his voice and his influence being raised for his bleeding and distracted country? Has his influence been brought to bear officially, socially, politically, or in any way, for the suppression of the rebellion? If so, I am unaware of it. Where is the evidence of devotion to his country in his speeches and in his votes? Where the evidence of the disposition on his part to overthrow and put down the rebellion? I have been told, Mr. President, by honorable gentlemen, as an evidence of the senator's devotion to his country and his great opposition to this Southern movement, that they heard him, and perhaps with tears in his eyes, remonstrate with the leaders of the rebellion that they should not leave him here in the Senate, or that they should not persist in their course after the relations that had existed between them and him, and the other Democrats of the country; that he thought they were treating him badly. This was the kind of remonstrance he made. Be it

* Mr. Sherman.

so. I am willing to give the senator credit for all he is entitled to, and I would to God I could credit him with more.

"But do senators remember that, when this battle was being fought in the Senate, I stood here on this side, solitary and alone, on the 19th day of December, 1860, and proclaimed that the Government was at an end if you denied it the power to enforce its laws? I declared, then, that a government which had not the power to coerce obedience on the part of those who violated the law was no government at all, and had failed to carry out the objects of its creation, and was, *ipso facto*, dissolved. When I stood on this floor and fought the battle for the supremacy of the Constitution and the enforcement of the laws, has the Senate forgotten that a bevy of conspirators gathered in from the other House, and that those who were here crowded around, with frowns and scowls, and expressions of indignation and contempt towards me, because I dared to raise my feeblè voice in vindication of the Constitution and the enforcement of the laws of the Union? Have you forgotten the taunts, the jeers, the derisive remarks, the contemptuous expressions that were indulged in? If you have, I have not. If the senator felt such great reluctance at the departure from the Senate of the chiefs of the rebellion, I should have been glad to receive one encouraging smile from him when I was fighting the battles of the country. I did not receive one encouraging expression; I received not a single sustaining look. It would have been peculiarly encouraging to me, under the circumstances, to be greeted and encouraged by one of the senator's talents and long standing in public life: but he was cold as an iceberg, and I stood solitary and alone amidst the gang of conspirators that had gathered around me. So much for the senator's remonstrances and expressions of regret for the retirement of those gentlemen.

"The bearing of the senator since he wrote this letter has not been unobserved. I have not compared notes; I have not hunted up the record in reference to it; but I have a perfect recollection of it. Did we not see, during the last session of Congress, the line being drawn between those who were devoted to the Union and those who were not? Cannot we sometimes see a great deal more than is expressed? Does it require us to have a man's sentiments written down in burning and blazing characters, before we are able to judge what they are? Has it not been observable all through this history where the true Union heart has stood? What was the senator's bearing at the last session of Congress? Do we not know that in the main he stood here opposed substantially to every measure which was necessary to sustain the Government in its trial and peril? He may perhaps have voted for some measures that were collateral, remote, indirect in their bearing; but do we not know that his vote and his influence were cast against the measures which were absolutely necessary to sustain the Government in its hour of peril?

"Some gentlemen have said, and well said, that we should not judge by party. I say so, too. I voted to let the senator from Indiana into the body, and as a Democrat my bias and prejudice would rather be in his favor. I am a Democrat now; I have been one all my life; I expect to live and die one; and the corner-stone of my Democracy rests upon the enduring basis of the Union. Democrats may come and go; but they shall never divert me from the polar star by which I have ever been guided from early life—the great principle of Democracy upon which this Government rests, and which cannot be carried out without the preservation of the Union of these States. The pretence hitherto employed by many who are now in the traitors' camp has been, 'We are for the Union; we are not for dissolution; but we are opposed to coercion.' How long, senators, have you heard that siren song? Where are now most of those who sang those siren tones to us? Look back to the last session, and inquire where now are the men who then were singing that song in our ears? Where is Trusten Polk, who then stood here so gently craving for peace? He is in the rebel camp. Where is John C. Breckinridge?—a man for whose promotion to the Presidency I did what I could, physically, mentally, and pecuniarily; but when he satisfied me that he was for breaking up this Government, and would ere long be a traitor to his country, I dropped him as I would the senator from Indiana. He was here at the last session of Congress; and everybody could see then that he was on the road to the traitors' camp. Instead of sustaining the Government, he, too, was crying out for peace; but he was bitter against 'Lincoln's government.' Sir, when I talk about preserving this great Government, I do not have its executive officer in my mind. The executive head of the Government comes in and goes out of office every four years. He is the mere creature of the people. I talk about the Government without regard to the particular executive officers who have charge of it. If they do well, we can continue them; if they do wrong, we can turn them out. Mr. Lincoln having come in according to the forms of law and the Constitution, I, loving my Government and the Union, felt it to be my duty to stand by the Government, and to stand by the Administration in all those measures that I believed to be necessary and proper for the preservation and perpetuation of the Union.

"Mr. Polk has gone; Mr. Breckinridge has gone; my namesake, the late senator from Missouri, has gone. Did you not see the line of separation at the last session? Although senators make speeches in which they give utterance to disclaimers, we can see their bearing. It is visible now; and the obligations of truth and duty to my country require me to speak of it. I believe there are treasonable tendencies here now; and how long it will be before they will lead to the traitors' camp, I shall not undertake to say. The great point with these gentlemen is, that they are opposed to coercion and to the enforcement of the laws. Without regard to the general bearing of the senator from Indiana upon that point, let me quote the conclusion of his letter of the 7th of September, 1861, to J. Fitch. I will read only the concluding portion of the letter, as it does him no injustice to omit the remainder:

"'And hence I have opposed, and so long as my present convictions last shall continue to oppose the entire coercive policy of the Government. I hope this may be satisfactory to my friends. For my enemies I care not.'

"Does not this correspond with the senator's general bearing? Has he given his aid, or countenance, or influence in any manner towards the efforts of the Government to sustain itself? What has been his course? We know that great stress has been laid upon the word 'coercion,' and it has been played upon effectually for the purpose of prejudicing the Southern mind, in connection with the other term, 'subjugation of the States,' which has been used so often. We may as well be honest and fair, and admit the truth of the great proposition, that a government cannot exist—in other words, it is no government—if it is without the power to enforce its laws and coerce obedience to them. That is all there is of it; and the very instant you take that power from this Government, it is at an end; it is a mere rope of sand that will fall to pieces of its own weight. It is idle, utopian, chimerical, to talk about a government existing without the power to enforce its laws. How is the Government to enforce its laws? The Constitution says that Congress shall have power 'to provide for calling forth the militia to execute the laws of the Union, suppress insurrections, and repel invasions.' Let me ask the senator from Indiana, with all his astuteness, how is rebellion to be put down, how is it to be resisted, unless there is some power in the Government to enforce its laws?

"If there be a citizen who violates your post-office laws, who counterfeits the coin of the United States, or who commits any other offence against the laws of the United States, you subject him to trial and punishment. Is not that coercion? Is not that enforcing the laws? How is rebellion to be put down without coercion, without enforcing the laws? Can it be done? The Constitution provides that—

"'The United States shall guarantee to every State in this Union a republican form of government, and shall protect each of them from invasion; and on application of the Legislature, or of the Executive (when the Legislature cannot be convened), against domestic violence.'

"How is this Government to put down domestic violence in a State without coercion? How is the nation to be protected against insurrection without coercing the citizens to obedience? Can it be done? When the senator says he is against the entire coercive policy of the Government, he is against the vital principle of all government. I look upon this as the most revolutionary and destructive doctrine that ever was preached. If this Government cannot call forth the militia, if it cannot repel invasion, if it cannot put down domestic violence, if it cannot suppress rebellion, I ask if the great objects of the Government are not at an end?

"Look at my own State, by way of illustration. There is open rebellion there; there is domestic violence; there is insurrection. An attempt has been made to transfer that State to another power. Let me ask the senator from Indiana if the Constitution does not require you to guarantee us a republican form of government in that State? Is not that your sworn duty? We ask you to put down this unholy rebellion. What answer would he give us? We ask you to protect us against insurrection and domestic violence. What is his reply? 'I am against your whole coercive policy; I am against the enforcement of the laws.' I say that if that principle be acted on, your Government is at an end; it fails utterly to carry out the object of its creation. Such a principle leads to the destruction of the Government, for it must inevitably result in anarchy and confusion. 'I am opposed to the entire coercive policy of the Government,' says the senator from Indiana. That cuckoo note has been reiterated to satiety; it is understood; men know the nature and character of their Government, and they also know that to cry out against 'coercion' and 'subjugation' is mere *ad captandum*, idle, and unmeaning slang-whanging.

"Sir, I may be a little sensitive on this subject upon the one hand, while I know I want to do ample justice upon the other. I took an oath to support the Constitution of the United States. There is rebellion in the land; there is insurrection against the authority of this Government. Is the senator from Indiana so unobservant or so obtuse that he does not know now that there has been a deliberate design for years to change the nature and character and genius of this Government? Do we not know that these schemers have been deliberately at work, and that there is a party in the South, with some associates in the North, and even in the West, that have become tired of free government, in which they have lost confidence? They raise an outcry against 'coercion,' that they may paralyze the Government, cripple the exercise of the great powers with which it was invested, and finally change its form and subject us to a Southern despotism. Do we not know it to be so? Why disguise this great truth? Do we not know that they have been anxious for a change of government for years? Since this rebellion commenced it has manifested itself in many quarters. How long is it since the organ of the Government at Richmond, the *Richmond Whig*, declared that rather than live under the Government of the United States, they preferred to take the constitutional Queen of Great Britain as their protector; that they would make an alliance with Great Britain for the purpose of preventing the enforcement of the laws of the United States? Do we not know this? Why then play 'hide and go seek?' Why say, 'Oh, yes, I am for the Union,' while every act, influence, conversation, vote, is against it? What confidence can we have in one who takes such a course?

"The people of my State, down-trodden and oppressed by the iron heel of Southern despotism, appeal to you for protection. They ask you to protect them against domestic violence. They want you to help them to put down this unholy and damnable rebellion. They call upon this Government for the execution of its constitutional duty to guarantee to them a republican form of government, and to protect them against the tyranny and despotism which is stalking abroad. What is the cold reply? 'I am against the entire coercive policy; I am not for enforcing the laws.' Upon such a doctrine government crumbles to pieces, and anarchy and despotism reign throughout the land.

"Indiana, God bless her, is as true to the Union as the needle is to the pole. She has sent out her 'columns;' she has sent her thousands into the field: for what? To sustain the Constitution and to enforce the laws; and as they march with strong arms and brave hearts to relieve a suffering people, who have committed no offence save devotion to this glorious Union; as they march to the rescue of the Constitution and to extend its benefits again to a people who love it dearly, and who have been ruthlessly torn from under its protecting ægis, what does their senator say to them? 'I am against the entire policy of coercion.' Do you ever hear a senator who thus talks make any objection to the exercise of unconstitutional and tyrannical power by the so-called Southern Confederacy, or say a word against its practice of coercion? In all the speeches that have been delivered on that point, has one sentence against usurpation, against despotism, against the exercise of doubtful and unconstitutional powers by that Confederacy, been uttered? Oh, no! Have you heard any objection to their practising not only coercion, but usurpation? Have they not usurped government? Have they not oppressed, and are they not now tyrannizing over the people? The people of my State are coerced, borne down, trodden beneath the iron heel of power. We appeal to you for protection. You stand by and see us coerced; you stand by and see tyranny triumphing, and no sympathy, no kindness, no helping hand can be extended to us. Your Government is paralyzed; your Government is powerless; that which you have called a government is a dream, an idle thing. You thought you had a government, but you have none. My people are appealing to you for protection under the Constitution. They are arrested by hundreds and by thousands; they are dragged away from their homes and incarcerated in dungeons. They ask you for protection. Why do you not give it? Some of them are lying chained in their lonely prison-house

The only response to their murmur is the rattling and clanking of the chains that bind their limbs. The only response to their appeals is the grating of the hinges of their dungeon. When we ask for help under the Constitution, we are told that the Government has no power to enforce the laws. Our people are oppressed and down-trodden, and you give them no remedy. They were taught to love and respect the Constitution of the United States. What is their condition to-day? They are hunted and pursued like the beasts of the forest by the secession and disunion hordes who are enforcing their doctrine of coercion. They are shot or hung for no crime save a desire to stand by the Constitution of the United States. Helpless children and innocent females are murdered in cold blood. Our men are hung and their bodies left upon the gibbet. They are shot and left lying in the gorges of the mountains; not even thrown into the caves there to lie, but are left exposed to pass through all the loathsome stages of decomposition, or to be devoured by the birds of prey. We appeal for protection, and are told by the senator from Indiana and others, 'We cannot enforce the laws; we are against the entire coercive policy.' Do you not hear their groans? Do you not hear their cries? Do you not hear the shrieks of oppressed and down-trodden women and children? Sir, their tones ring out so loud and clear, that even listening angels look from heaven in pity.

"I will not pursue this idea further, for I perceive that I am consuming more time than I intended to occupy. I think it is clear, without going further into the discussion, that the senator from Indiana has sympathized with the rebellion. The conclusion is fixed upon my mind that the senator from Indiana has disqualified himself, has incapacitated himself to discharge the duties in this body of a loyal senator. I think it is clear that, even if we were a court, we should be bound to convict him; but I do not narrow the case down to the close rules that would govern a court of justice.

"But, sir, in the course of the discussion one palliating fact was submitted by the distinguished senator from New Jersey,* and he knows that I do not refer to him in any spirit of unkindness. There was more of legal learning and special pleading in his suggestion than solidity or sound argument. He suggested that there was no proof that this letter had ever been delivered to Jefferson Davis, and that therefore the senator from Indiana ought not to be convicted. Well, sir, on the other hand, there is no proof that it was not delivered. It is true, the letter was found in Mr. Lincoln's possession; but who knows that Davis did not read the letter, and hand it back to Lincoln? It may have been that, being from his early friend, a man whom he respected, Lincoln desired to keep the letter and show it to somebody else. We have as much right to infer that the letter was delivered as that it was not; but be that as it may, does it lessen the culpability of the senator from Indiana? He committed the act, and so far as he was concerned it was executed. It would be no palliation of his offence if the man did not deliver the letter to Davis. The intent and the act were just as complete as if it had been delivored.

* Mr. Ten Eyck.

"During the war of the Revolution, in 1780, Major André, a British spy, held a conference with Benedict Arnold. Arnold prepared his letters, six in number, and they were handed over to Major André, who put them between the soles of his feet and his stockings, and he started on his way to join Sir Henry Clinton. Before he reached his destination, however, John Paulding and his two associates arrested Major André. They pulled off his boots and his stockings, and they got the papers; they kept them, and Major André was tried and hung as a spy. Arnold's papers were not delivered to Sir Henry Clinton; but is there anybody here who doubts that Arnold was a traitor? Has public opinion ever changed upon that subject? He was not convicted in a court, nor were the treasonable dispatches which were to expose the condition of West Point, and make the British attack upon it easy and successful, ever delivered to Sir Henry Clinton, and yet André was hung as a spy. Because Sir Henry Clinton did not receive the treasonable documents, was the guilt of Benedict Arnold any the less? I do not intend to argue this question in a legal way; I simply mention this circumstance by way of illustration of the point which has been urged in the present case, and leave it for the public judgment to determine.

"Sir, it has been said by the distinguished senator from Delaware* that the questions in controversy might all have been settled by compromise. He dealt rather extensively in the party aspect of the case, and seemingly desired to throw the *onus* of the present

* Mr. Saulsbury.

condition of affairs entirely on one side. He told us that if so and so had been done, these questions could have been settled, and that now there would have been no war. He referred particularly to the resolution offered during the last Congress by the senator from New Hampshire,* and upon the vote on that he based his argument. I do not mean to be egotistical; but if he will give me his attention, I intend to take the staple out of that speech, and show how much of it is left on that point.

"The speech of the senator from Delaware was a very fine one. I have not the power, as he has, to con over, and get by rote, and memorize handsomely rounded periods, and make a great display of rhetoric. It is my misfortune that I am not so skilled. I have to seize on fugitive thoughts as they pass through my mind, make the best application of them I can, and express them in my own crude way. I am not one of those who prepare rounding, sounding, bounding rhetorical flourishes, read them over twenty times before I come into the Senate Chamber, make a great display, and have it said, 'Oh, that is a fine speech!' I have heard many such fine speeches; but when I have had time to follow them up, I have found that it never took long to analyze them, and reduce them to their original elements; and that when they were reduced, there was not very much of them. [Laughter.]

"The senator told us that the adoption of the Clark amendment to the Crittenden resolutions defeated the settlement of the questions of controversy; and that,

* Mr. Clark.

but for that vote, all could have been peace and prosperity now. We were told that the Clark amendment defeated the Crittenden Compromise, and prevented a settlement of the controversy. On this point I will read a portion of the speech of my worthy and talented friend from California,* and when I speak of him thus, I do it in no unmeaning sense. I intend that he, not I, shall answer the senator from Delaware. I know that sometimes, when gentlemen are fixing up their pretty rhetorical flourishes, they do not take time to see all the sharp corners they may encounter. If they can make a readable sentence, and float on in a smooth, easy stream, all goes well, and they are satisfied. As I have said, the senator from Delaware told us that the Clark amendment was the turning-point in the whole matter ; that from it had flowed rebellion, revolution, war, the shooting and imprisonment of people in different States—perhaps he meant to include my own. This was the Pandora's box that has been opened, out of which all the evils that now afflict the land have flown. Thank God, I still have hope that all will yet be saved. My worthy friend from California, during the last session of Congress, made one of the best speeches he ever made. I bought five thousand copies of it for distribution, but I had no constituents to send them to [laughter] ; and they have been lying in your document-room ever since, with the exception of a few, which I thought would do good in some quarters. In the course of that speech upon this very point, he made use of these remarks :

* Mr. Latham.

"'Mr. President, being last winter a careful eye-witness of all that occurred, I soon became satisfied that it was a deliberate, wilful design, on the part of some representatives of Southern States, to seize upon the election of Mr. Lincoln merely as an excuse to precipitate this revolution upon the country. One evidence, to my mind, is the fact that South Carolina never sent her senators here.'

"Then they certainly were not influenced by the Clark amendment.

"'An additional evidence is, that when gentlemen on this floor, by their votes, could have controlled legislation, they refused to cast them, for fear that the very propositions submitted to this body might have an influence in changing the opinions of their constituencies. Why, sir, when the resolutions submitted by the senator from New Hampshire [Mr. Clark] were offered as an amendment to the Crittenden propositions, for the manifest purpose of embarrassing the latter, and the vote taken on the 16th of January, 1861, I ask, what did we see? There were fifty-five senators at that time upon this floor in person. The *Globe* of the second session, Thirty-sixth Congress, part 1, page 409, shows that upon the call of the yeas and nays immediately preceding the vote on the substituting of Mr. Clark's amendment, there were fifty-five votes cast. I will read the vote from the *Globe:*

"'YEAS.—Messrs. Anthony, Baker, Bingham, Cameron, Chandler, Clark, Collamer, Dixon, Doolittle, Durkee, Fessenden, Foot, Foster, Grimes, Hale, Harlan, King, Seward, Simmons, Sumner, Ten Eyck, Trumbull, Wade, Wilkinson, and Wilson—25.'

"'Nays.—Messrs. Bayard, Benjamin, Bigler, Bragg, Bright, Clingman, Crittenden, Douglas, Fitch, Green, Gwin, Hemphill, Hunter, Iverson, Johnson of Arkansas, Johnson of Tennessee, Kennedy, Lane, Latham, Mason, Nicholson, Pearce, Polk, Powell, Pugh, Rice, Saulsbury, Sebastian, Slidell, and Wigfall—30.'

"'The vote being taken immediately after, on the Clark proposition, was as follows :'

"'Yeas.—Messrs. Anthony, Baker, Bingham, Cameron, Chandler, Clark, Collamer, Dixon, Doolittle, Durkee, Fessenden, Foot, Foster, Grimes, Hale, Harlan, King, Seward, Simmons, Sumner, Ten Eyck, Trumbull, Wade, Wilkinson, and Wilson—25.

"'Nays.—Messrs. Bayard, Bigler, Bragg, Bright, Clingman, Crittenden, Fitch, Green, Gwin, Hunter, Johnson of Tennessee, Kennedy, Lane, Latham, Mason, Nicholson, Pearce, Polk, Powell, Pugh, Rice, Saulsbury, and Sebastian—23.'

"'Six senators retained their seats and refused to vote, thus themselves allowing the Clark proposition to supplant the Crittenden resolution by a vote of twenty-five to twenty-three. Mr. Benjamin, of Louisiana; Mr. Hemphill and Mr. Wigfall, of Texas; Mr. Iverson, of Georgia; Mr. Johnson, of Arkansas, and Mr. Slidell, of Louisiana, were in their seats, but refused to cast their votes.'

"I sat right behind Mr. Benjamin, and I am not sure that my worthy friend was not close by, when he refused to vote, and I said to him, 'Mr. Benjamin, why do you not vote? Why not save this proposition, and see if we cannot bring the country to it?' He gave me rather an abrupt answer, and said he would control his own action without consulting me or anybody else. Said I, 'Vote, and show yourself an honest man.' As soon as the vote was taken, he and others telegraphed South, 'We cannot get any compromise.' Here were six Southern men refusing to vote, when the amendment would have been rejected by four majority if they had voted. Who, then, has brought these evils on the country? Was it Mr. Clark? He was acting out his own policy; but with the help we had from the other side of the chamber, if all those on this side had been true to the Constitution and faithful to their constituents, and had acted with fidelity to the country, the amendment of the senator from New Hampshire could have been voted down, the defeat of which, the senator from Delaware says, would have saved the country. Whose fault was it? Who is responsible for it? Who did it? Southern traitors, as was said in the speech of the senator from California. They did it. They wanted no compromise. They accomplished their object by withholding their votes; and hence the country has been involved in the present difficulty. Let me read another extract from this speech of the senator from California:

"'I recollect full well the joy that pervaded the faces of some of those gentlemen at the result, and the sorrow manifested by the venerable senator from Kentucky (Mr. Crittenden). The record shows that Mr. Pugh, from Ohio, despairing of any compromise between the extremes of ultra republicanism and disunionists, working manifestly for the same end, moved, immediately after the vote was announced, to lay the whole subject on the table. If you will turn to page 443, in the same volume, you will find, when, at a late period, Mr. Cameron, from Pennsylvania, moved to reconsider the vote, appeals having been made to sustain those who were struggling to preserve the peace of the country, that the vote *was* reconsidered; and when, at last, the Crittenden propositions were submitted on the 2d day of March, these Southern States having nearly all seceded, they were then lost by but one vote. Here is the vote:

"'YEAS.—Messrs. Bayard, Bigler, Bright, Crittenden, Douglas, Gwin, Hunter, Johnson of Tennessee, Kennedy, Lane, Latham, Mason, Nicholson, Polk, Pugh, Rice, Sebastian, Thomson, and Wigfall—19.

"'NAYS.—Messrs. Anthony, Bingham, Chandler, Clark, Dixon, Doolittle, Durkee, Fessenden, Foot, Foster, Grimes, Harlan, King, Morrill, Sumner, Ten Eyck, Trumbull, Wade, Wilkinson, and Wilson—20.'

"'If these seceding Southern senators had remained, there would have passed, by a large vote (as it did without them), an amendment, by a two-thirds vote, forbidding Congress ever interfering with slavery in the States. The Crittenden proposition would have been indorsed by a majority vote, the subject finally going before the people, who have never yet, after consideration, refused justice, for any length of time, to any portion of the country.

"'I believe more, Mr. President, that these gentlemen were acting in pursuance of a settled and fixed plan to break up and destroy this Government.'

"When we had it in our power to vote down the amendment of the senator from New Hampshire, and adopt the Crittenden resolutions, certain Southern senators prevented it; and yet, even at a late day of the session, after they had seceded, the Crittenden proposition was only lost by one vote. If rebellion and bloodshed and murder have followed, to whose skirts does the responsibility attach? I summed up all these facts myself in a speech during the last session; but I have preferred to read from the speech of the senator from California, he being better authority, and having presented the facts better than I could.

"What else was done at the very same session? The House of Representatives passed, and sent to this body, a proposition to amend the Constitution of the United States, so as to prohibit Congress from ever hereafter interfering with the institution of slavery in the States, making that restriction a part of the organic law of the land. That constitutional amendment came here after the senators from seven States had seceded; and yet it was passed by a two-thirds vote in the Senate. Have you ever heard of any one of the States which had then seceded, or which has since seceded, taking up that amendment to the Constitution, and saying they would ratify it, and make it a part of that instrument? No. Does not the whole history of this rebellion tell you that it was revolution that the leaders wanted, that they started for, that they intended to have? The facts to which I have referred show how the Crittenden proposition might have been carried; and when the senators from the Slave States were reduced to one-fourth of the members of this body, the two Houses passed a proposition to amend the Constitution, so as to guarantee to the States perfect security in regard to the institution of slavery in all future time, and prohibiting Congress from legislating on the subject.

"But what more was done? After Southern senators had treacherously abandoned the Constitution and deserted their posts here, Congress passed bills for the organization of three new territories—Dakotah, Nevada, and Colorado; and in the sixth section of each of those bills, after conferring, affirmatively, power on the Territorial Legislature, it went on to exclude certain powers by using a negative form of expression; and it provided, among other things, that the Legislature should have no power to legislate so as to impair the right to private property; that it should lay no tax discriminating against one description of property in favor of another; leaving the power on all these questions, not in the Territorial Legislature, but in the people when they should come to form a State constitution.

"Now, I ask, taking the amendment to the Constitution, and taking the three territorial bills, embracing every square inch of territory in the possession of the United States, how much of the slavery question was left? What better compromise could have been made? Still, we are told that matters might have been compromised; and that if we had agreed to compromise, bloody rebellion would not now be abroad in the land. Sir, Southern senators are responsible for it. They stood here with power to accomplish the result, and yet treacherously, and, I may say, tauntingly, they left this chamber, and announced that they had dissolved their connection with the Government. Then, when we were left in the hands of those whom we had been taught to believe would encroach upon our rights, they gave us, in the constitutional amendment and in the three territorial bills, all that had ever been asked; and yet gentlemen talk about compromise! Why was not this taken and accepted?

"No; it was not compromise that the leaders wanted; they wanted power; they wanted to destroy this Government, so that they might have place and emolument for themselves. They had lost confidence in the intelligence, and virtue, and integrity of the people, and their capacity to govern themselves; and they intended to separate and form a government, the chief corner-stone of which should be slavery, disfranchising the great mass of the people, of which we have seen constant evidence, and merging the powers of government in the hands of the few. I know what I say. I know their feelings and their sentiments. I served in the Senate here with them. I know they were a close corporation, that had no more confidence in or respect for the people than has the Dey of Algiers. I fought that close corporation here. I knew that they were no friends of the people. I knew that Slidell, and Mason, and Benjamin, and Iverson, and Toombs were the enemies of free government, and I know so now. I commenced the war upon them before a State seceded; and I intend to keep on fighting this great battle before the country for the perpetuity of free government. They seek to overthrow it, and to establish a despotism in its place. That is the great battle which is upon our hands. The great interests of civil liberty and free government call upon every patriot and every lover of popular rights to come forward and discharge his duty.

"We see this great struggle; we see that the exercise of the vital principle of government itself is denied by those who desire our institutions to be overthrown and despotism established on their ruins If we have not the physical and moral courage to exclude from our midst men whom we believe to be unsafe depositories of public power and public trust,—men whose associates were rolling off honeyed accents against coercion, and are now in the traitors' camp,—if we have not the courage to force these men from our midst, because we have known them, and have been personal friends with them for years, we are not entitled to sit here as senators ourselves. Can you expect your brave men, your officers and soldiers who are now in 'the tented field,' subject to all the hardships and privations pertaining to a civil war like this, to have courage, and to march on with patriotism to crush treason on every battle-field, when you have not the courage to expel it from your midst? Set those brave men an example; say to them by your acts and voice that you evidence your intention to put down traitors in the field by ejecting them from your midst, without regard to former associations.

"I do not say these things in unkindness. I say them in obedience to duty, a high constitutional duty that I owe to my country; yes, sir, that I owe to my wife and children. By your failure to exercise the powers of this Government, by your failure to enforce the laws of the Union, I am separated from those most dear to me. Pardon me, sir, for this personal allusion. My wife and children have been turned into the street, and my house has been turned into a barrack; and for what? Because I stand by the Constitution and the institutions of the country that I have been taught to love, respect, and venerate. This is my offence. Where are my sons-in-law? One to-day is lying in prison; another is forced to fly to the mountains to evade the pursuit of the hell-born and hell-bound conspiracy of disunion and secession; and when their cries come up here to you for protection, we are told, 'No; I am against the entire coercive policy of the Government.'

"The speech of the senator from California, the other day, had the effect in some degree, and seemed to be intended to give the question a party tinge. If I know myself,—although, as I avowed before, I am a Democrat, and expect to live and die one,—I know no party in this great struggle for the existence of my country. The argument presented by the senator from California was that we need not be in such hot pursuit of Mr. Bright, or those senators who entertain his sentiments, who are still here, because we had been a little dilatory in expelling other traitorous senators heretofore; and he referred us to the resolution of the senator from Maine,* which was introduced at the special session in March last, declaring that certain senators having withdrawn, and their seats having thereby become vacant, the secretary should omit their names from the roll of the Senate. I know there seemed to be a kind of timidity, a kind of fear, to make use of the word 'expel' at that time; but the fact that we declared the seats vacant, and stopped there, did not preclude us from afterwards passing a vote of censure. The resolution, which was adopted in March, merely stated the fact that senators had withdrawn, and left their seats vacant. At the next session a resolution

* Mr. Fessenden.

was introduced to expel the other senators from the seceded States who did not attend in the Senate; and my friend* moved to strike out of that very resolution the word 'expelled,' and insert 'vacated;' so that I do not think he ought to be much offended at it. I simply allude to it to show how easy it is for us to forget the surrounding circumstances that influenced our action at the time it took place. We know that a year ago there was a deep and abiding hope that the rebellion would not progress as it has done; that it would cease; and that there might be circumstances which, at one time, would to some extent justify us in allowing a wide margin which, at another period of time, would be wholly unjustifiable.

"All this, however, amounts to nothing. We have a case now before us that requires our action, and we should act upon it conscientiously in view of the facts which are presented. Because we neglected to expel traitors before, and omitted to have them arrested, and permitted them to go away freely, and afterwards declared their seats vacant because they had gone, we are not now prevented from expelling a senator who is not worthy to be in the Senate. I do not say that other traitors may not be punished yet. I trust in God the time will come, and that before long, when these traitors can be overtaken, and we may mete out to them condign punishment, such as their offence deserves. I know who was for arresting them. I know who declared their conduct to be treason. Here in their midst I told them it was treason, and they might make the best of it they could.

* Mr. Latham.

"Sir, to sum up the argument, I think there is but little in the point presented by the senator from New Jersey, of there being no proof of the reception of the letter; and I think I have extracted the staple commodity entirely out of the speech of the senator from Delaware; and so far as the force of the argument, based upon the Senate having at one session expelled certain members, while at the previous session it only vacated their seats, is concerned, I think the senator from California answers that himself. As to the polished and ingenious statement of the case made by the senator from New York,* I think I have answered that by putting the case upon a different basis from the one presented by him, which seems to control his action.

"Mr. President, I have alluded to the talk about compromise. If I know myself, there is no one who desires the preservation of this Government more than I do; and I think I have given as much evidence as mortal man could give of my devotion to the Union. My property has been sacrificed; my wife and children have been turned out of doors; my sons have been imprisoned; my son-in-law has had to run to the mountains; I have sacrificed a large amount of bonds in trying to give some evidence of my devotion to the Government under which I was raised. I have attempted to show you that, on the part of the leaders of this rebellion, there was no desire to compromise: compromise was not what they wanted; and now the great issue before the country is the perpetuation or the destruction of free government. I have shown

* Mr. Harris.

how the resolution of the venerable senator from Kentucky* was defeated, and that Southern men are responsible for that defeat—six sitting in their places and refusing to vote. His proposition was only lost by two votes; and in the end, when the seceders had gone, by only one. Well do I remember, as was described by the senator from California, the sadness, the gloom, the anguish that played over his venerable face when the result was announced; and I went across the chamber, and told him that here were men refusing to vote, and that to me was administered a rebuke by one of them for speaking to him on the subject.

"Now, the senator from Delaware tells us that if that compromise had been made, all these consequences would have been avoided. It is a mere pretence; it is false. Their object was to overturn the Government. If they could not get the control of this Government, they were willing to divide the country and govern a part of it. Talk not of compromise now. What, sir, compromise with traitors with arms in their hands! Talk about 'our Southern brethren' when they present their swords at your throats and their bayonets at your bosoms! Is this a time to talk about compromise? Let me say, and I regret that I have to say it, that there is but one way to compromise this matter, and that is to crush the leaders of this rebellion and put down treason. You have got to subdue them; you have got to conquer them; and nothing but the sacrifice of life and blood will do it. The issue is made. The leaders of rebellion have decreed

* Mr. Crittenden.

eternal separation between you and them. Those leaders must be conquered, and a new set of men brought forward who are to vitalize and develop the Union feeling in the South. You must show your courage here as senators, and impart it to those who are in the field. If you were now to compromise, they would believe that they could whip you one to five, and you could not live in peace six months, or even three months. Settle the question now; settle it well; settle it finally; crush out the rebellion and punish the traitors. I want to see peace, and I believe that is the shortest way to get it. Blood must be shed, life must be sacrificed, and you may as well begin at first as last. I only regret that the Government has been so tardy in its operations. I wish the issue had been met sooner. I believe that if we had seen as much in the beginning as we see to-day, this rebellion would have been wound up and peace restored to the land by this time.

"But let us go on; let us encourage the army and the navy; let us vote the men and the means necessary to vitalize and to bring into requisition the enforcing and coercive power of the Government; let us crush out the rebellion, and anxiously look forward to the day—God grant it may come soon—when that baleful comet of fire and of blood that now hovers over this distracted people may be chased away by the benignant star of peace. Let us look forward to the time when we can take the flag, the glorious flag of our country, and nail it below the cross, and there let it wave as it waved in the olden time, and let us gather around it, and inscribe as our motto, 'Liberty and Union, now and forever, one and inseparable.'

Let us gather around it, and while it hangs floating beneath the cross, let us exclaim, 'Christ first, our country next.' Oh, how gladly rejoiced I should be to see the dove returning to the ark with the olive-leaf, indicating that land was found, and that the mighty waters had abated. I trust the time will soon come when we can do as they did in the olden times, when the stars sang together in the morning, and all creation proclaimed the glory of God. Then let us do our duty in the Senate and in the councils of the nation, and thereby stimulate our brave officers and soldiers to do theirs in the field.

"Mr. President, I have occupied the attention of the Senate much longer than I intended. In view of the whole case, without personal unkind feeling towards the senator from Indiana, I am of opinion that duty to myself, duty to my family, duty to the Constitution, duty to the country, obedience to the public judgment, all require me to cast my vote to expel Mr. Bright from the Senate, and when the occasion arrives I shall so record my vote."

CHAPTER VI.

APPEAL TO THE PEOPLE OF TENNESSEE.

"FELLOW-CITIZENS :—Tennessee assumed the form of a body politic, as one of the United States of America, in the year seventeen hundred and ninety-six, at once entitled to all the privileges of the Federal Constitution, and bound by all its obligations. For nearly sixty-five years she continued in the enjoyment of all her rights, and in the performance of all her duties, one of the most loyal and devoted of the sisterhood of States. She had been honored by the elevation of two of her citizens to the highest place in the gift of the American people, and a third had been nominated for the same high office, who received a liberal though ineffective support. Her population had rapidly and largely increased, and their moral and material interests correspondingly advanced. Never was a people more prosperous, contented, and happy than the people of Tennessee under the Government of the United States, and none less burdened for the support of the authority by which they were protected. They felt their Government only in the conscious enjoyment of the benefits it conferred and the blessings it bestowed.

"Such was our enviable condition until within the

year just past, when, under what baneful influences it is not my purpose now to inquire, the authority of the Government was set at defiance, and the Constitution and laws contemned, by a rebellious, armed force. Men who, in addition to the ordinary privileges and duties of the citizen, had enjoyed largely the bounty and official patronage of the Government, and had, by repeated oaths, obligated themselves to its support, with sudden ingratitude for the bounty and disregard of their solemn obligation, engaged, deliberately and ostentatiously, in the accomplishment of its overthrow. Many, accustomed to defer to their opinions and to accept their guidance, and others, carried away by excitement or overawed by seditious clamor, arrayed themselves under their banners, thus organizing a treasonable power, which, for the time being, stifled and suppressed the authority of the Federal Government.

"In this condition of affairs it devolved upon the President, bound by his official oath to preserve, protect, and defend the Constitution, and charged by the law with the duty of suppressing insurrection and domestic violence, to resist and repel this rebellious force by the military arm of the Government, and thus to re-establish the Federal authority. Congress, assembling at an early day, found him engaged in the active discharge of this momentous and responsible trust. That body came promptly to his aid, and while supplying him with treasure and arms to an extent that would previously have been considered fabulous, they, at the same time, with almost absolute unanimity, declared 'that this war is not waged on their part in any spirit of oppression, nor for any purpose of conquest or subjugation, nor purpose of overthrowing or interfering with the rights or the established institutions of these States; but to defend and maintain the supremacy of the Constitution and to preserve the Union, with all the dignity, equality, and rights of the several States unimpaired; and that as soon as these objects are accomplished, the war ought to cease.' In this spirit, and by such co-operation, has the President conducted this mighty contest, until, as Commander-in-Chief of the Army, he has caused the national flag again to float undisputed over the capitol of our State. Meanwhile the State government has disappeared. The Executive has abdicated; the Legislature has dissolved; the Judiciary is in abeyance. The great ship of state, freighted with its precious cargo of human interests and human hopes, its sails all set, and its glorious old flag unfurled, has been suddenly abandoned by its officers and mutinous crew, and left to float at the mercy of the winds, and to be plundered by every rover upon the deep. Indeed the work of plunder has already commenced. The archives have been desecrated; the public property stolen and destroyed; the vaults of the State Bank violated, and its treasures robbed, including the funds carefully gathered and consecrated for all time to the instruction of our children.

"In such a lamentable crisis the Government of the United States could not be unmindful of its high constitutional obligation to guarantee to every State in this Union a republican form of government, an obligation which every State has a direct and immediate interest in having observed towards every other State; and from which, by no action on the part of the people in any State, can the Federal Government be absolved. A republican form of government, in consonance with the Constitution of the United States, is one of the fundamental conditions of our political existence, by which every part of the country is alike bound, and from which no part can escape. This obligation the national Government is now attempting to discharge. I have been appointed, in the absence of the regular and established State authorities, as Military Governor for the time being, to preserve the public property of the State, to give the protection of law actively enforced to her citizens, and, as speedily as may be, to restore her government to the same condition as before the existing rebellion.

"In this grateful but arduous undertaking, I shall avail myself of all the aid that may be afforded by my fellow-citizens. And for this purpose I respectfully but earnestly invite all the people of Tennessee, desirous or willing to see a restoration of her ancient government, without distinction of party affiliations or past political opinions or action, to unite with me, by counsel and co-operative agency, to accomplish this great end. I find most, if not all of the offices, both State and Federal, vacated, either by actual abandonment, or by the action of the incumbents in attempting to subordinate their functions to a power in hostility to the fundamental law of the State, and subversive of her national allegiance. These offices must be filled temporarily, until the State shall be restored so far to its accustomed quiet, that the people can peaceably assemble at the ballot-box and select agents of their own choice. Otherwise anarchy would prevail, and no man's life or property would be safe from the desperate and unprincipled.

"I shall therefore, as early as practicable, designate for various positions under the State and county governments, from among my fellow-citizens, persons of probity and intelligence, and bearing true allegiance to the Constitution and Government of the United States, who will execute the functions of their respective offices until their places can be filled by the action of the people. Their authority, when their appointment shall have been made, will be accordingly respected and observed.

"To the people themselves the protection of the Government is extended. All their rights will be duly respected, and their wrongs redressed when made known. Those who through the dark and weary night of the rebellion have maintained their allegiance to the Federal Government will be honored. The erring and misguided will be welcomed on their return. And while it may become necessary, in vindicating the violated majesty of the law, and in reasserting its imperial sway, to punish intelligent and conscious treason in high places, no merely retaliatory or vindictive policy will be adopted. To those especially who, in a private, unofficial capacity, have assumed an attitude of hostility to the Government, a full and complete amnesty for all past acts and declarations is offered, upon the one condition of their again yielding themselves peaceful citizens to the just supremacy of the laws. This I advise them to do for their own good, and for the peace and welfare of our beloved State, endeared to me by the associations of long and active years, and by the enjoyment of her highest honors.

"And appealing to my fellow-citizens of Tennessee, I point you to my long public life as a pledge for the sincerity of my motives, and an earnest for the performance of my present and future duties."

CHAPTER VII.

NOMINATED FOR THE VICE-PRESIDENCY.

After sustaining, by voice and vote in the Senate, every measure calculated to secure a Federal triumph over the Southern Confederacy, President Lincoln appointed Andrew Johnson Military Governor of Tennessee, in the early spring of 1862. This appointment, with the rank of brigadier-general, was confirmed by the Senate on the 5th of March, and he immediately left Washington for Nashville, and entered upon his new and responsible position. No appointment could be more appropriate, and the country soon felt that the right man was indeed in the right place. Every proclamation, every address, every act received general and hearty approbation, and in the desperate siege sustained by Nashville against a strong Confederate force in the autumn of the same year, the governor was first and foremost in aiding and encouraging the defenders of the city. "I am not a soldier, he said, "but I will shoot any one who talks of surrender." His conduct as Governor of Tennessee, added to his former course in the Senate, so increased his popularity among the Northern masses, that on the 6th of June, 1864, he was unanimously nominated by the Union Convention, assembled at Baltimore, as the candidate for the Vice-Presidency of the United States. On accepting the nomination he addressed to the committee the following clear and comprehensive communication:

"NASHVILLE, TENN., *July* 2, 1864.

"HON. WILLIAM DENNISON, *Chairman, and others, Committee of the National Union Convention:*

"GENTLEMEN: Your communication of the 9th ult., informing me of my nomination for the Vice-Presidency of the United States by the National Convention held at Baltimore, and inclosing a copy of the resolutions adopted by that body, was not received until the 25th ult.

"A reply on my part had been previously made to the action of the convention in presenting my name, in a speech delivered in this city on the evening succeeding the day of the adjournment of the convention, in which I indicated my acceptance of the distinguished honor conferred by that body, and defined the grounds upon which that acceptance was based, substantially saying what I now have to say. From the comments made upon that speech by the various presses of the country to which my attention has been directed, I considered it to be regarded as a full acceptance.

"In view, however, of the desire expressed in your communication, I will more fully allude to a few points that have been heretofore presented.

"My opinions on the leading questions at present agitating and distracting the public mind, and especially in reference to the rebellion now being waged against the Government and authority of the United States, I presume are generally understood. Before the Southern people assumed a belligerent attitude (and repeatedly since), I took occasion most frankly to declare the views I then entertained in relation to the wicked purposes of the Southern politicians. They have since undergone but little, if any, change. Time and subsequent events have rather confirmed than diminished my confidence in their correctness.

"At the beginning of this great struggle I entertained the same opinion of it I do now, and in my place in the Senate I denounced it as treason, worthy the punishment of death, and warned the Government and people of the impending danger. But my voice was not heard or counsel heeded until it was too late to avert the storm. It still continued to gather over us without molestation from the authorities at Washington, until at length it broke with all its fury upon the country. And now, if we would save the Government from being overwhelmed by it, we must meet it in the true spirit of patriotism, and bring traitors to the punishment due their crime, and, *by force of arms*, crush out and subdue the last vestige of rebel authority in every State. I felt then, as now, that the destruction of the Government was deliberately determined upon by wicked and designing conspirators, whose lives and fortunes were pledged to carry it out; and that no compromise, short of an unconditional recognition of the independence of the Southern States could have been, or could now be proposed, which they would accept. The clamor for 'Southern Rights,' as the rebel journals were pleased to designate their rallying cry, was not to secure their assumed rights *in the Union and under the Constitution*, but to disrupt the Government, and establish an independent organization, based upon slavery, which they could at all times control.

"The separation of the Government has for years past been the cherished purpose of the Southern leaders. Baffled in 1832 by the stern, patriotic heroism of Andrew Jackson, they sullenly acquiesced, only to mature their diabolical schemes, and await the recurrence of a more favorable opportunity to execute them. Then the pretext was the tariff, and Jackson, after foiling their schemes of nullification and disunion, with prophetic perspicacity warned the country against the renewal of their efforts to dismember the Government.

"In a letter, dated May 1, 1833, to the Rev. A. J. Crawford, after demonstrating the heartless insincerity of the Southern nullifiers, he said: 'Therefore the tariff was only a pretext, and disunion and a Southern Confederacy the real object. The next pretext will be the negro or slavery question.'

"Time has fully verified this prediction, and we have now not only 'the negro or slavery question,' as the pretext, but the real cause of the rebellion, and both must go down together. It is vain to attempt to reconstruct the Union with the distracting element of slavery in it. Experience has demonstrated its incompatibility with free and republican government, and it would be unwise and unjust longer to continue it as one of the institutions of the count y. While it remained subordinate to the Constitution and laws of the United States, I yielded to it my support; but when it became rebellious, and attempted to rise above the Government, and control its action, I threw my humble influence against it.

"The authority of the Government is supreme, and will admit of no rivalry. No institution can rise above it, whether it be slavery or any other organized power. In our happy form of government all must be subordinate to the will of the people, when reflected through the Constitution and laws made pursuant thereto, State or Federal. This great principle lies at the foundation of every Government, and cannot be disregarded without the destruction of the Government itself. In the support and practise of correct principles we can never reach wrong results; and by rigorously adhering to this great fundamental truth, the end will be the preservation of the Union, and the overthrow of an institution which has made war upon and attempted the destruction of the Government itself.

"The mode by which this great change—the emancipation of the slave—can be effected, is properly found in the power to amend the Constitution of the United States. This plan is effectual and of no doubtful authority; and while it does not contravene the timely exercise of the war-power by the President in his emancipation proclamation, it comes stamped with the authority of the people themselves, acting in accordance with the written rule of the supreme law of the land, and must therefore give more general satisfaction and quietude to the distracted public mind.

"By recurring to the principles contained in the

resolutions so unanimously adopted by the convention, I find that they substantially accord with my public acts and opinions heretofore made known and expressed, and are therefore most cordially indorsed and approved, and the nomination, having been conferred without any solicitation on my part, is with the greater pleasure accepted.

"In accepting the nomination I might here close, but I cannot forego the opportunity of saying to my old friends of the Democratic party *proper*, with whom I have so long and pleasantly been associated, that the hour has now come when that great party can justly vindicate its devotion to true Democratic policy and measures of expediency. The war is a war of great principles. It involves the supremacy and life of the Government itself. If the rebellion triumphs, free government—North and South—fails. If, on the other hand, the Government is successful—as I do not doubt—its destiny is fixed, its basis permanent and enduring, and its career of honor and glory just begun. In a great contest like this for the existence of free government, the path of duty is patriotism and principle. Minor considerations and questions of administrative policy should give way to the higher duty *of first preserving the Government;* and then there will be time enough to wrangle over the men and measures pertaining to its administration.

"This is not the hour for strife and division among ourselves. Such differences of opinion only encourage the enemy, prolong the war, and waste the country. Unity of action and concentration of power should be our watchword and rallying cry. This accomplished, the time will rapidly approach when their armies in the field—that great power of the rebellion—will be broken and crushed by our gallant officers and brave soldiers; and ere long they will return to their homes and firesides to resume again the avocations of peace, with the proud consciousness that they have aided in the noble work of re-establishing upon a surer and more permanent basis the great temple of American Freedom.

"I am, gentlemen, with sentiments of high regard,

"Yours truly,

"ANDREW JOHNSON."

CHAPTER VIII.

TAKES THE OATH AS PRESIDENT.

At the warmly contested election on the 14th of November, 1864, all the States voting, except three, gave a majority of their suffrages for Lincoln and Johnson; and when, on the 4th of March, 1865, the Vice-President elect took his seat as presiding officer of the Senate, he could already see the end of the conflict in which he had borne so active and memorable a part. It must have been to him an occasion full of just satisfaction and honorable pride. As he looked around the chamber whose walls had so often echoed with the tones of his rebuke of secession doctrines and secession acts, as he saw the vacant seats of a score of his former associates who were now wandering fugitives, his bosom must indeed have swelled with the cheering consciousness that, at least in his case, an honest and brave defence of principle had been rightly rewarded by the applause and gratitude of his country. But Providence had not destined him to remain in the quiet and pleasant office to which he had been called by the suffrages of the nation. A wider sphere of honor, of usefulness, and of responsibility was thrown upon him by one of the most sad and startling catastrophes in the wide sweep of human history. On the 14th of April, only six days after the close of the civil war by the surrender of General Lee and the army of Northern Virginia, Abraham Lincoln fell by the hand of an assassin, and a few hours after his mournful departure Andrew Johnson, in accordance with the provisions of the Constitution, was inducted into the exalted position of President of the United States.

After the customary oath had been administered by the Chief-Justice, President Johnson delivered the following feeling and pertinent address:

"GENTLEMEN—I must be permitted to say that I have been almost overwhelmed by the announcement of the sad event which has so recently occurred. I feel incompetent to perform duties so important and responsible as those which have been so unexpectedly thrown upon me. As to an indication of any policy which may be pursued by me in administration of the Government, I have to say, that that must be left for development as the administration progresses. The message or declaration must be made by the acts as they transpire. The only assurance that I can now give of the future, is by reference to the past. The course which I have taken in the past, in connection with this rebellion, must be regarded as a guaranty of the future. My past public life, which has been long and laborious, has been founded, as I in good conscience believe, upon a great principle of right, which lies at the basis of all things. The best energies of my life have been spent in endeavoring to establish and perpetuate the principles of free government, and I believe that the Government, in passing through its present trials, will settle down upon principles consonant with popular rights more permanent and enduring than heretofore. I must be permitted to say, if I understand the feelings of my own heart, I have long labored to ameliorate and alleviate the condition of the great mass of the American people. Toil and an honest advocacy of the great principles of free government, have been my lot. The duties have been mine—the consequences are God's. This has been the foundation of my political creed. I feel that in the end the Government will triumph, and that these great principles will be permanently established.

"In conclusion, gentlemen, let me say that I want your encouragement and countenance. I shall ask and rely upon you and others in carrying the Government through its present perils. I feel, in making this request, that it will be heartily responded to by you, and all other patriots and lovers of the rights and interests of a free people."

CHAPTER IX.

RECEPTION OF THE ILLINOIS DELEGATION.

On the 18th of April, 1865, a delegation of citizens of Illinois paid their respects to President Johnson, at his rooms in the Treasury Building.

Governor Oglesby presented the delegation, and made the subjoined address:—

"Mr. President:—I take much pleasure in presenting to you this delegation of the citizens of Illinois, representing almost every portion of the State. We are drawn together by the mournful events of the past few days, to give some feeble expression to the feelings we, in common with the whole nation, realize as pressing us to the earth, by appropriate and respectful ceremonies. We thought it not inappropriate before we should separate, even in this sad hour, to seek this interview with your Excellency, that, while the bleeding heart is pouring out its mournful anguish over the death of our beloved late President, the idol of our State and the pride of the whole country, we may earnestly express to you, the living head of this nation, our deliberate, full, and abiding confidence in you as the one who, in these dark hours, must bear upon yourself the mighty responsibility of maintaining, defending, and directing its affairs. In the midst of this sadness, through the oppressive gloom that surrounds us, we look to you and to a bright future for our country. The assassination of the President of the United States deeply depresses and seriously aggravates the entire nation; but under our blessed Constitution it does not delay, nor for any great length of time retard, its progress; does not for an instant disorganize or threaten its destruction. The record of your whole past life, familiar to all, the splendor of your recent gigantic efforts to stay the hand of treason and assassination, and restore the flag to the uttermost bounds of the Republic, assure that noble State which we represent, and, we believe, the people of the United States, that we may safely trust our destinies in your hands; and to this end we come, in the name of the State of Illinois, and, we confidently believe, fully and faithfully expressing the wishes of our people, to present and pledge to you the cordial, earnest, and unremitting purpose of our State to give your administration the strong support we have heretofore given to the administration of our lamented late President, the policy of whom we have heretofore, do now, and shall continue to indorse."

THE PRESIDENT'S REPLY.

President Johnson replied as follows:—

"GENTLEMEN:—I have listened with profound emotion to the kind words you have addressed to me. The visit of this large delegation to speak to me through you, sir, these words of encouragement, I had not anticipated. In the midst of the saddening circumstances which surround us, and the immense responsibility thrown upon me, an expression of the confidence of individuals, and still more of an influential body like that before me, representing a great commonwealth, cheers and strengthens my heavily burdened mind. I am at a loss for words to respond. In an hour like this, of deepest sorrow, were it possible to embody in words the feelings of my bosom, I could not command my lips to utter them. Perhaps the best reply I could make, and the one most readily appropriate to your kind assurances of confidence, would be to receive them in silence. [Sensation.] The throbbings of my heart since the sad catastrophe which has appalled us cannot be reduced to words; and, oppressed as I am with the new and great responsibility which has devolved upon me, and saddened with grief, I can with difficulty respond to you at all. But I cannot permit such expression of the confidence reposed in me by the people to pass without acknowledgment. To an individual like myself, who has never claimed much, but who has, it is true, received from a generous people many marks of trust and honor for a long time, an occasion like this and a manifestation of public feeling so well-timed are peculiarly acceptable. Sprung from the people myself, every pulsation of the popular heart finds an immediate answer in my own. By many men in public life such occasions are often considered merely formal. To me they are real. Your words of countenance and encouragement sank deep in my heart, and were I even a coward I could not but gather from them strength to carry out my convictions of right. Thus feeling, I shall enter upon the discharge of my great duty firmly, steadfastly [applause], if not with the signal ability exhibited by my predecessor, which is still fresh in our sorrowing minds. Need I repeat that no heart feels more sensibly than mine this great affliction? In what I say on this occasion I shall indulge in no petty spirit of anger, no feeling of revenge. But we have beheld a notable event in the history of mankind. In the midst of the American people, where every citizen is taught to obey law and observe the rules of Christian conduct, our Chief Magistrate, the beloved of all hearts, has been assassinated; and when we trace this crime to its cause, when we remember the source whence the assassin drew his inspiration, and then look at the result, we stand yet more astounded at this most barbarous, most diabolical assassination. Such a crime as the murder of a great and good man, honored and revered, the beloved and the hope of the people, springs not alone from a solitary individual of ever so desperate wickedness. We can trace its cause through successive steps, without my enumerating them here, back to that source which is the spring of all our woes. No one can say that if the perpetrator of this fiendish deed be arrested he should not undergo the extremest penalty the law knows for crime; none will say that mercy should interpose. But is he alone guilty? Here, gentlemen, you perhaps expect me to present some indication of my future policy. One thing I will say. Every era teaches its lesson. The times we live in are not without instruction. The American people must be taught—if they do not already feel—

that treason is a crime, and must be punished [applause]; that the Government will not always bear with its enemies; that it is strong, not only to protect, but to punish. [Applause.] When we turn to the criminal code and examine the catalogue of crimes, we there find arson laid down as a crime with its appropriate penalty; we find there theft and robbery and murder given as crimes; and there, too, we find the last and highest of crimes—treason. [Applause.] With other and inferior offences our people are familiar. But in our peaceful history treason has been almost unknown. The people must understand that it is the blackest of crimes, and will be surely punished. [Applause.] I make this allusion, not to excite the already exasperated feelings of the public, but to point out the principles of public justice which should guide our action at this particular juncture, and which accord with sound public morals. Let it be engraven on every heart that treason is a crime, and traitors shall suffer its penalty. [Applause.] While we are appalled, overwhelmed at the fall of one man in our midst by the hand of a traitor, shall we allow men—I care not by what weapons—to attempt the life of a State with impunity? While we strain our minds to comprehend the enormity of this assassination, shall we allow the nation to be assassinated? [Applause.] I speak in no spirit of unkindness. I leave the events of the future to be disposed of as they arise, regarding myself as the humble instrument of the American people. In this, as in all things, justice and judgment shall be determined by them. I do not harbor bitter or revengeful feelings towards any. In general terms, I would say that public morals and public opinion should be established upon the sure and inflexible principles of justice. [Applause.] When the question of exercising mercy comes before me, it will be considered calmly, judicially—remembering that I am the Executive of the nation. I know men love to have their names spoken of in connection with acts of mercy; and how easy it is to yield to this impulse! But we must not forget that what may be mercy to the individual is cruelty to the State. [Applause.] In the exercise of mercy there should be no doubt left that this high prerogative is not used to relieve a few at the expense of the many. Be assured that I shall never forget that I am not to consult my own feelings alone, but to give an account to the whole people. [Applause.] In regard to my future course I will now make no professions, no pledges. I have been connected somewhat actively with public affairs, and to the history of my past public acts, which is familiar to you, I refer for those principles which have governed me heretofore, and will guide me hereafter. In general, I will say I have long labored for the amelioration and elevation of the great mass of mankind. My opinions as to the nature of popular government have long been cherished; and constituted as I am, it is now too late in life for me to change them. I believe that government was made for man, not man for government. [Applause.] This struggle of the people against the most gigantic rebellion the world ever saw has demonstrated that the attachment of the people to their Government is the strongest national defence human wisdom can devise. [Applause.] So long as each man feels that the interests of the Government are his interests; so long as the public heart turns in the right direction, and the people understand and appreciate the theory of our Government and love liberty, our Constitution will be transmitted unimpaired. If the time ever comes when the people shall fail, the Government will fail, and we shall cease to be one of the nations of the earth. After having preserved our form of free government, and shown its power to maintain its existence through the vicissitudes of nearly a century, it may be that it was necessary for us to pass through this last ordeal of intestine strife to prove that this Government will not perish from internal weakness, but will stand to defend itself against all foes and punish treason. [Applause.] In the dealings of an inscrutable Providence and by the operation of the Constitution, I have been thrown unexpectedly into this position. My past life, especially my course during the present unholy rebellion, is before you. I have no principles to retract; I defy any one to point to any of my public acts at variance with the fixed principles which have guided me through life. I have no professions to offer. Professions and promises would be worth nothing at this time. No one can foresee the circumstances that will hereafter arise. Had any man, gifted with prescience four years ago, uttered and written down in advance the events of this period, they would have seemed more marvellous than any thing in the 'Arabian Nights.' I shall not attempt to anticipate the future. As events occur, and it becomes necessary for me to act, I shall dispose of each as it arises, deferring any declaration or message until it can be written, paragraph by paragraph, in the light of events as they transpire."

The members of the delegation were then severally introduced to the President by Governor Oglesby.

CHAPTER X.

RECEPTION OF THE BRITISH AMBASSADOR.

On the 20th of April, 1865, Sir Frederick A. Bruce, Envoy Extraordinary and Minister Plenipotentiary of Her Britannic Majesty to the United States Government, presenting his credentials to the President, spoke as follows :

"Mr. President :—It is with deep and sincere concern that I have to accompany my first official act with expressions of condolence. On Saturday last the ceremony that takes place here to-day was to have been performed, but the gracious intentions of the late lamented President were frustrated by the events which have plunged this country in consternation and affliction, and which will call forth in Great Britain feelings of horror, as well as of profound sympathy. It becomes, therefore, my duty, sir, to present the letter from my sovereign, of which I am the bearer, to you, as President of the United States; and it is with pleasure that I convey the assurances of regard and good-will which her Majesty entertains towards you, sir, as President of the United States. I am further directed to express her Majesty's friendly disposition towards the great nation of which you are Chief Magistrate, and her hearty good wishes for its peace, prosperity, and welfare. Her Majesty has nothing more at heart than to conciliate those relations of amity and good understanding which have so long and so happily existed between the two kindred nations of the United States and Great Britain, and it is in this spirit that I am directed to perform the duties of the important and honorable post confided to me. Permit me, sir, to say, that it shall be the object of my earnest endeavors to carry out my instructions faithfully in this respect, and to express the hope, sir, that you will favorably consider my attempts to merit your approbation, and to give effect to the friendly intentions of the Queen and of her Majesty's Government. I have the honor to place in your hands the letter of credence confided to me by her Majesty."

THE PRESIDENT'S REPLY.

To which President Johnson replied:

"SIR FREDERICK A. BRUCE:—The very cordial and friendly sentiments which you have expressed on the part of her Britannic Majesty give me great pleasure. Great Britain and the United States, by the extended and various forms of commerce between them, the contiguity of portions of their possessions, and the similarity of their language and laws, are drawn into constant and intimate intercourse. At the same time they are, from the same causes, exposed to frequent occasions of misunderstanding, only to be averted by mutual forbearance. So eagerly are the people of the two countries engaged, throughout almost the whole world, in the pursuit of similar commercial enterprises, accompanied by natural rivalries and jealousies, that, at first sight, it would almost seem that the two Governments must be enemies, or at best cold and calculating friends. So devoted are the two nations throughout all their domain, and even in their most remote territory and colonial possessions, to the principles of civil rights and constitutional liberty, that, on the other hand, the superficial observer might erroneously count upon a continued concert of action and sympathy, amounting to an alliance between them. Each is charged with the development of the progress of the human race, and each in its sphere is subject to difficulties and trials not participated in by the other. The interests of civilization and of humanity require that the two should be friends. I have always known and accounted as a fact, honorable to both countries, that the Queen of England is a sincere and honest well-wisher to the United States. I have been equally frank and explicit in the opinion that the friendship of the United States towards Great Britain is enjoined by all considerations of interest and of sentiment affecting the character of both. You will, therefore, be accepted as a minister friendly and well-disposed to the maintenance of peace and the honor of both countries. You will find myself and all my associates acting in accordance with the same enlightened policy and consistent sentiments, and so I am sure that it will not occur in your case that either yourself or this Government will ever have cause to regret that such an important relationship existed at such a crisis.

CHAPTER XI.

RECEPTION OF THE DIPLOMATIC CORPS.

Soon after the reception of the British Minister, the members of the Diplomatic Corps were presented to President Johnson, when Baron Von Gerolt addressed the President as follows :—

"Mr. President :—The representatives of foreign nations have assembled here to express to your Excellency their feelings at the deplorable event of which they have been witnesses ; to say how sincerely they share the national mourning for the cruel fate of the late President, Abraham Lincoln, and how deeply they sympathize with the Government and people of the United States in their great affliction. With equal sincerity we tender to you, Mr. President, our best wishes for the welfare and prosperity of the United States, and for your personal health and happiness. May we be allowed, also, Mr. President, to give utterance on this occasion to our sincerest hopes for an early re-establishment of peace in this great country, and for the maintenance of the friendly relations between the Government of the United States and the Governments which we represent ?"

REPLY OF THE PRESIDENT.

To which the President replied :—

"GENTLEMEN OF THE DIPLOMATIC BODY :—I heartily thank you, on behalf of the Government and people of the United States, for the sympathy which you have so feelingly expressed upon the mournful event to which you refer. The good wishes also which you kindly offer for the welfare and prosperity of the United States, and for my personal health and happiness, are gratefully received. Your hopes for the early restoration of peace in this country are cordially reciprocated by me, and you may be assured that I shall leave nothing undone towards preserving those relations of friendship which now fortunately exist between the United States and all foreign powers."

CHAPTER XII.

ADDRESS TO LOYAL SOUTHERNERS.

During the same month a deputation of loyal men from various Southern States waited on the President. In reply to a brief address, he said:—

"It is hardly necessary for me on this occasion to say that my sympathies and impulses, in connectien with this nefarious Rebellion, beat in unison with yours. Those who have passed through this bitter ordeal, and who participated in it to a great extent, are more competent, as I think, to judge and determine the true policy which should be pursued. [Applause.] I have but little to say on this question in response to what has been said. It enunciates and expresses my own feelings to the fullest extent, and in much better language than I can at the present moment summon to my aid. The most that I can say is, that, entering upon the duties that have devolved upon me under circumstances that are perilous and responsible, and being thrown into the position I now occupy unexpectedly, in consequence of the sad event, the heinous assassination which has taken place—in view of all that is before me and the circumstances that surround me—I cannot but feel that your encouragement and kindness are peculiarly acceptable and appropriate. I do not think you, who have been familiar with my course,—you who are from the South,—deem it necessary for me to make any professions as to the future on this occasion, nor to express what my course will be upon questions that may arise. If my past life is no indication of what my future will be, my professions were both worthless and empty; and in returning you my sincere thanks for this encouragement and sympathy, I can only reiterate what I have said before, and, in part, what has just been read. As far as clemency and mercy are concerned, and the proper exercise of the pardoning power, I think I understand the nature and character of the latter. In the exercise of clemency and mercy, that pardoning power should be exercised with caution. I do not give utterance to my opinions on this point in any spirit of revenge or unkind feelings. Mercy and clemency have been pretty large ingredients in my composition, having been the Executive of a State, and thereby placed in a position in which it was necessary to exercise clemency and mercy. I have been charged with going too far, being too lenient, and have become satisfied that mercy without justice is a crime, and that when mercy and clemency are exercised by the Executive, it should always be done in view of justice, and in that manner alone is properly exercised that great prerogative. The time has come, as you who have had to drink this bitter cup are fully aware, when the American people should be made to understand the true nature of crime. Of crime generally our people have a high understanding, as well as of the necessity for its punishment; but in the catalogue of crimes there is one, and that the highest known to the laws and the Constitution, of which, since the days of Jefferson and Aaron Burr, they have become oblivious. That is—treason. Indeed, one who has become distinguished in treason and in this Rebellion said, that 'when traitors become numerous enough, treason becomes respectable; and to become a traitor, was to constitute a portion of the aristocracy of the country.' God protect the people against such an aristocracy. Yes, the time has come when the people should be taught to understand the length and breadth, the depth and height of treason. An individual occupying the highest position among us was lifted to that position by the free offering of the American people,—the highest position on the habitable globe. This man we have seen, revered, and loved,—one who, if he erred at all, erred ever on the side of clemency and mercy,—that man we have seen Treason strike, through a fitting instrument, and we have beheld him fall like the bright star falling from its sphere. Now, there is none but would say, if the question came up, what should be done with the individual who assassinated the Chief Magistrate of the nation,—He is but a man—one man, after all. But if asked what should be done with the assassin, what should be the penalty, the forfeit exacted? I know what response dwells in every bosom. It is, that he should pay the forfeit with his life. And hence we see there are times when mercy and clemency, without justice, become a crime. The one should temper the other, and bring about that proper means. And if we should say this when the case was the simple murder of one man by his fellow-man, what should we say when asked what should be done with him, or them, or those, who have raised impious hands to take away the life of a nation composed of thirty millions of people? What would be the reply to that question? But while in mercy we remember justice, in the language that has been uttered, I say, justice towards the leaders, the conscious leaders; but I also say amnesty, conciliation, clemency, and mercy to the thousands of our countrymen whom you and I know have been deceived or driven into this infernal Rebellion. And so I return to where I started from, and again repeat that it is time our people were taught to know that treason is a crime, not a mere political difference, not a mere contest between two parties, in which one succeeded and the other has simply failed. They must know it is treason; for if they had succeeded, the life of the nation would have been reft from it,—the Union would have been destroyed. Surely the Constitution sufficiently defines treason. It consists in levying war against the United States, and in giving their enemies aid and comfort. With this definition it requires the exercise of no great acumen to ascertain who are traitors. It requires no great perception to tell who have levied war against the United States; nor does it require any great stretch of reasoning to ascertain who has given aid to the enemies of the United States; and when the Government of the United States does ascertain who are the conscious and intelligent traitors, the penalty and the forfeit should be paid. [Applause.] I know how to appreciate the condition of being driven from one's home. I can sympathize with him whose all has been taken from him,—with him who has been denied the place that gave his children birth. But let us, withal, in the restoration of true government, proceed temperately and dispassionately, and hope and pray that the time will come, as I believe, when all can return and remain at our homes, and treason and traitors be driven from our land [applause], when again law and order shall reign, and the banner of our country be unfurled over every inch of territory within the area of the United States. [Applause.] In conclusion, let me thank you most profoundly for this encouragement and manifestation of your regard and respect, and assure you that I can give no greater assurance regarding the settlement of this question, than that I intend to discharge my duty, and in that way which shall, in the earliest possible hour, bring back peace to our distracted country. And I hope the time is not far distant when our people can all return to their homes and firesides, and resume their various avocations."

CHAPTER XIII.

SPEECH TO THE INDIANA DELEGATION.

At the close of the month of April, 1865, the President spoke as follows, in response to an address from a delegation from the State of Indiana:—

"As my honorable friend (Governor Morton) knows, I long since took the ground that this Government was sent upon a great mission among the nations of the earth; that it had a great work to perform, and that in starting it, it was started in perpetuity. Look back for one single moment to the Articles of Confederation, and then come down to 1787, when the Constitution was formed—what do you find? That we, 'the People of the United States, in order to form a more perfect government,' etc. Provision is made for the admission of new States, to be added to the old ones embraced within the Union. Now, turn to the Constitution; we find that amendments may be made by a recommendation of two-thirds of the members of Congress, if ratified by three-fourths of the States. Provision is made for the admission of new States; no provision is made for the secession of old ones. The instrument was made to be good in perpetuity, and you can take hold of it, not to break up the

Government, but to go on perfecting it more and more as it runs down the stream of time. We find the Government composed of integral parts. An individual is an integer, and a State itself is an integer, and the various States form the Union, which is itself an integer, they all making up the Government of the United States. Now we come to the point of my argument, so far as concerns the perpetuity of the Government. We have seen that the Government is composed of parts, each essential to the whole, and the whole essential to each part. Now, if an individual (part of a State) declare war against the whole, in violation of the Constitution, he, as a citizen, has violated the law, and is responsible for the act as an individual. There may be more than one individual; it may go on until they become parts of States. Sometimes the rebellion may go on increasing in number till the State machinery is overturned, and the country becomes like a man that is paralyzed on one side. But we find in the Constitution a great panacea provided. It provides that the United States (that is, the great integer) shall guarantee to each State (the integers composing the whole) in this Union a republican form of government. Yes, if rebellion has been rampant, and set aside the machinery of a State for a time, there stands the great law to remove the paralysis, and revitalize it and put it on its feet again. When we come to understand our system of government, though it be complex, we see how beautifully one part moves in harmony with another; then we see our Government is to be a perpetuity, there being no provision for pulling it down, the Union being its vitalizing power, imparting life to the whole of the States that move around it like planets around the sun, receiving thence light, and heat, and motion. Upon this idea of destroying States, my position has been heretofore well known, and I see no cause to change it now, and I am glad to hear its reiteration on the present occasion. Some are satisfied with the idea that States are to be lost in territorial and other divisions ; are to lose their character as States. But their life-breath has only been suspended, and it is a high constitutional obligation we have to secure each of these States in the possession and enjoyment of a republican form of government. A State may be in the Government with a peculiar institution, and by the operation of rebellion lose that feature ; but it was a State when it went into rebellion, and when it comes out without the institution, it is still a State. I hold it a solemn obligation in any one of these States where the rebel armies have been beaten back or expelled, I care not how small the ship of state, I hold it, I say, a high duty to protect and to secure to them a republican form of government. This is no new opinion. It is expressed in conformity with my understanding of the genius and theory of our Government. Then, in adjusting and putting the Government upon its legs again, I think the progress of this work must pass into the hands of its friends. If a State is to be nursed until it again gets strength, it must be nursed by its friends, not smothered by its enemies. Now, permit me to remark, that while I have opposed dissolution and disintegration on the one hand, on the other I am equally opposed to consolidation, or the centralization of power in the hands of a few.

CHAPTER XIV.

A DELEGATION OF SOUTHERN MEN VISIT THE PRESIDENT.

One of the most interesting episodes which has occurred since Mr. Johnson became President, probably took place in a spontaneous visit made by a number of prominent and distinguished Southern gentlemen, who happened to be in Washington on business. The significance of this visit arose from the fact that there was nothing of a political character to it, but was prompted solely by that respect which Mr. Johnson's honorable and humane course had inspired in the hearts of the Southern people. Where they had been apprehensive of revenge, they found kindness. Where they had looked for severity, they found gentleness. Animated by such feelings, those gentlemen determined to pay Mr. Johnson such a call as would be a surprise.

He was informed the day previous that some Southern gentlemen desired to pay their respects to him, and the hour at which it would be agreeable for him to receive them was fixed. The next day, September 11, accordingly, the gentlemen repaired to the White House, and meeting in the

East Room, organized themselves into a formal delegation. Mr. Phillips, of Alabama, was called to the chair. Judge Lockrane, of Georgia, stated that their object was to pay a visit of courtesy to the President, and express to him their unqualified confidence in the justice and magnanimity of the Government in the matter of reconstruction. On motion, Messrs. Bliss, of Alabama; McFarland, of Virginia; White, of Texas; Cannon, of South Carolina; Bass, of Arkansas; Wilkins, of Mississippi; Lockrane, of Georgia, and Baker, of Florida, were designated to individually present to the President such persons as were present from their respective States. The delegation was admitted soon after eleven o'clock, and presented to the President as follows, by Mr. McFarland, of Virginia:

"MR. PRESIDENT—The gentlemen accompanying me, and whom I have the honor of introducing to you, constitute a number of the most respectable citizens of nine of the Southern States. They come, sir, for the purpose of manifesting the sincere respect and regard they entertain for you, and to express their sincere determination to co-operate with you in whatever shall tend to promote the interests and welfare of our common country, and to say that they are as earnest now, and faithful to their allegiance to the United States and to the Constitution of the Union as in the past, and that they have great confidence in your wisdom to heal the wounds that have been made, and in your disposition to exercise all the leniency which can be commended by a sound and judicious policy. That they are assured, in doing this, of your desire and intention to sustain and maintain Southern rights in the union of the United States."

The President was surprised at the imposing appearance of the delegation, and was evidently much affected in reply. Every gesture and utterance was full of subdued eloquence. The reply was as follows:

"GENTLEMEN—I can only say, in reply to the remarks of your chairman, that I am highly gratified to receive the assurances he has given me. They are more than I could have expected under the circumstances. I must say I was unprepared to receive so numerous a delegation on this occasion; it was unexpected; I had no idea it was to be so large, or represent so many States. When I expressed as I did my willingness to see at any time so many of you as chose to do me the honor to call upon me, and stated that I should be gratified at receiving any manifestations of regard you might think proper to make, I was totally unprepared for any thing equal to the present demonstration. I am free to say it excites in my mind feelings and emotions that language is totally inadequate to express. When I look back upon my past actions, and recall a period scarcely more than four short years ago, when I stood battling for principles which many of you opposed and thought were wrong, I was battling for the same principles that actuate me to-day, and which principles, I thank my God, you have come forward on this occasion to manifest a disposition to support. I say now, as I have said on many former occasions, that I entertain no personal resentments, enmities, or animosities to any living soul south of Mason and Dixon's line, however much he may have differed from me in principle. The stand I then took I claim to have been the only true one. I remember how I stood pleading with my Southern brethren, when they stood with their hats in their hands ready to turn their backs upon the United States; how I implored them to stand with me there, and maintain our rights and fight our battles under the laws and Constitution of the United States. I think now, as I thought then, and endeavored to induce them to believe, that our true position was under the law and under the Constitution of the Union, with the institution of slavery in it; but if that principle made an issue that rendered a disintegration possible—if that made an issue which should prevent us from transmitting to our children a country as bequeathed to us by our fathers—I had nothing else to do but to stand by the Government, be the consequences what they might. I said then, what you all know, that I was for the institutions of the country as guaranteed by the Constitution, but above all things I was for the Union of the States. I remember the taunts, the jeers, the scowls with which I was treated. I remember the circle that stood around me, and remember the threats and intimidations that were freely uttered by the men who opposed me, and whom I wanted to befriend and guide by the light that led me; but feeling conscious in my own integrity, and that I was right, I heeded not what they might say or do to me, and was inspired and encouraged to do my duty regardless of aught else, and have lived to see the realization of my predictions, and the fatal error of those whom I vainly essayed to save from the results I could not but foresee. Gentlemen, we have passed through this rebellion. I say we, for it was we who are responsible for it. Yes, the South made the issue, and I know the nature of the Southern people well enough to know that when they have become convinced of an error, they frankly acknowledge it in a manly, open, direct manner ; and now, in the performance of that duty, or, indeed, in any act they undertake to perform, they do it heartily and frankly ; and now that they come to me, I understand them as saying that, 'We made the issue. We set up the Union of the States against the institution of slavery. We selected as arbitrator the God of battles; the arbitrament was the sword. The issue was fairly and honorably met. Both the questions presented have been settled against us, and we are prepared to accept the issue.' I find on all sides this spirit of candor and honor prevailing. It is said by all : 'The issue was ours, and the judgment has been given against us ; and the decision having been made against us, we feel bound in honor to abide by the arbitrament. In doing this we are doing ourselves no dishonor, and should not feel humiliated or degraded, but rather that we are ennobling ourselves by our action ; and we should feel that the Government has treated us magnanimously, and meet the Government upon the terms it has so magnanimously proffered us.'

"So far as I am concerned, personally, I am uninfluenced by any question, whether it affects the North or the South, the East or the West. I stand where I did of old, battling for the Constitution and the union of these United States. In doing so I know I opposed some of you gentlemen of the South when this doctrine of secession was being urged upon the country, and the declaration of your right to break up the Government and disintegrate the Union was made. I stand to-day, as I have ever stood, firmly in the opinion that if a monopoly contends against this country, the monopoly must go down, and the country must go up. Yes, the issue was made by the South against the Government, and the Government has triumphed; and the South, true to her instincts of frankness and manly honor, comes forth and expresses her willingness to abide the result of the decision in good faith. While I think that the rebellion has been arrested and subdued, and am happy in the consciousness of a duty well performed, I want not only you, but the people of the world to know, that while I dreaded and feared disintegration of the States, I am equally opposed to consolidation or concentration of power here, under whatever guise or name; and if the issue is forced upon us, I shall still endeavor to pursue the same efforts to dissuade from this doctrine of running to extremes: but I say, let the same rules be applied. Let the Constitution be our guide. Let the preservation of that and the union of the States be our principal aim. Let it be our hope that the Government may be perpetual, and that the principles of the Government, founded as they are on right and justice, may be handed down without spot or blemish to our posterity. As I have before remarked to you, I am gratified to see so many of you here to-day. It manifests a spirit I am pleased to observe. I know it has been said of me that my asperities are sharp, that I had vindictive feelings to gratify, and that I should not fail to avail myself of the opportunities that would present themselves to gratify such despicable feelings. Gentlemen, if my acts will not speak for me and for themselves, then any professions I might now make would be equally useless. But, gentlemen, if I know myself, as I think I do, I know that I am of the Southern people, and I love them and will do all in my power to restore them to that state of happiness and prosperity which they enjoyed before the madness of misguided men, in whom they had reposed their confidence, led them astray to their own undoing. If there is any thing that can be done on my part, on correct principles, on the principles of the Constitution, to promote these ends, be assured it shall be done. Let me assure you, also, that there is no disposition on the part of the Government to deal harshly with the Southern people. There may be speeches published from various quarters that may breathe a different spirit. Do not let them trouble or excite you, but believe that it is, as it is, the great object of the Government to make the union of these United States more complete and perfect than ever, and to maintain it on constitutional principles, if possible, more firmly than it has ever before been. Then, why cannot we all come up to the work in a proper spirit? In other words, let us look to the Constitution. The issue has been made and decided; then, as wise men—as men who see right and are determined to follow it as fathers and brothers, and as men who love their country in this hour of trial and suffering—why cannot we come up and help to settle the questions of the hour and adjust them according to the principles of honor and of justice? The institution of slavery is gone. The former status of the negro had to be changed, and we, as wise men, must recognize so patent a fact and adapt ourselves to circumstances as they surround us. [Voices, 'We are willing to do so. Yes, sir, we are willing to do so.'] I believe you are. I believe when your faith is pledged, when your consent has been given, as I have already said, I believe it will be maintained in good faith, and every pledge or promise fully carried out. [Cries, 'It will.'] All I ask or desire of the South or the North, the East or the West, is to be sustained in carrying out the principles of the Constitution. It is not to be denied that we have been great sufferers on both sides. Good men have fallen on both sides, and much misery is being endured as the necessary result of so gigantic a contest. Why, then, cannot we come together, and around the common altar of our country heal the wounds that have been made? Deep wounds have been inflicted. Our country has been scarred all over. Then, why cannot we approach each other upon principles which are right in themselves, and which will be productive of good to all? The day is not distant when we shall feel like some family that have had a deep and desperate feud, the various members of which have come together and compared the evils and sufferings they had inflicted upon each other. They had seen the influence of their error and its result, and, governed by a generous spirit of conciliation, they had become mutually forbearing and forgiving, and returned to their old habits of fraternal kindness, and become better friends than ever.

Then let us consider that the feud which alienated us has been settled and adjusted to our mutual satisfaction, and that we come together to be bound by firmer bonds of love, respect, and confidence than ever. The North cannot get along without the South, nor the South from the North, the East from the West, nor the West from the East; and I say it is our duty to do all that in our power lies to perpetuate and make stronger the bonds of our Union, seeing that it is for the common good of all that we should be united. I feel that this Union, though but the creation of a century, is to be perpetuated for all time, and that it cannot be destroyed except by the all-wise God who created it. Gentlemen, I repeat, I sincerely thank you for the respect manifested on this occasion, and for the expressions of approbation and confidence please accept my sincere thanks."

Mr. McFarland replied as follows:

"MR. PRESIDENT: On behalf of this delegation I return you my sincere thanks for your kind, generous—aye, magnanimous—expressions of kindly feeling towards the people of the South."

The remarks of the President, so full of kindly feeling and generous confidence, were frequently interrupted with applause; and it is doubtful whether, among all the interviews which Mr. Johnson has had with Southern men since the termination of the war, there has been one whom the bright and nobler traits of his character have shown out more conspicuously, or one which made so deep and so lasting an impression on the Southern mind. In this they read the language of the *heart*—always, after all, more to be relied upon and trusted than the cold, intellectual responses of the head, be they never so unexceptionable or satisfactory.

CHAPTER XV.

VETO OF THE FREEDMEN'S BUREAU BILL.

THERE is no trait of human character more thoroughly worthy of respect than consistency. So common is the yielding both in private and public life to feelings of expediency, of interest, of personal and political prejudices and antipathies, that to see a man acting under all circumstances with a firm and steady adherence to principle is sure to excite admiration. The present age can afford no grander example of this noble virtue than the conduct of President Johnson in his policy of again restoring to its full life and healthful action the broken and disordered members of the once glorious Federal Union. He early took the ground that the secession of a State was an entire impossibility, that an ordinance declaring it was in its every conception null and voïd, and that upon the close of armed opposition to the General Government the States engaged in it resumed, as a matter of course, their original position. The Congress in session at the commencement of the late civil war took the same view of the subject, when, after the first terrible defeat of Manassas, it unanimously adopted a resolution to the effect that the war was not waged for the purpose of interfering in any manner with the rights of the States, nor with their domestic institutions, but solely and entirely for the preservation and restoration of the Union itself. The present Congress, however, refuses to abide by the act of its predecessor, and though hostilities have long since ceased, the late insurgent States are denied all State attributes, and condemned to the painful and ignominious fate of conquered provinces. This stand of Congress, directly in opposition to the well-known opinions of the President, has brought out all the independence and energy of his character in a manner calculated to electrify the people, and to cause them to rely with the utmost confidence upon his capacity to restore once again the unity, the prosperity, and the happiness of the country.

An opportunity was afforded him in his famous veto of the Freedmen's Bureau Bill, and his speech in response to the congratulations of his countrymen upon that auspicious event, to proclaim to the whole world the strength of his convictions, the purity of his patriotism, and the indomitable power and courage of his soul. We give these remarkable utterances in full; for no sketch of President Johnson can be complete without this crowning evidence of the wonderful consistency of his political career:

"Constant as the Northern Star;
Of whose true, fix'd, and resting quality
There is no fellow in the firmament."

"TO THE SENATE OF THE UNITED STATES:

"I have examined with care the bill which originated in the Senate, and has been passed by the two Houses of Congress, to amend an act entitled 'An act to establish a bureau for the relief of freedmen and refugees, and for other purposes.' Having, with much regret, come to the conclusion that it would not be consistent with the public welfare to give my approval to the measure, I return the bill to the Senate with my objections to its becoming a law.

"I might call to mind, in advance of these objections, that there is no immediate necessity for the proposed measure. The act to establish a bureau for the relief of freedmen and refugees, which was approved in the month of March last, has not yet expired. It was thought stringent and extensive enough for the purpose in view. Before it ceases to have effect, further experience may assist to guide us to a wise conclusion as to the policy to be adopted in time of peace.

"I have, with Congress, the strongest desire to secure to the freedmen the full enjoyment of their freedom and their property and their entire independence and equality in making contracts for their labor. But the bill before me contains provisions which, in my opinion, are not warranted by the Constitution and are not well suited to accomplish the end in view. The bill proposes to establish by authority of Congress military jurisdiction over all parts of the United

States containing refugees and freedmen. It would, by its very nature, apply with most force to those parts of the United States in which the freedmen most abound ; and it expressly extends the existing temporary jurisdiction of the Freedmen's Bureau, with greatly enlarged powers, over those States in which the ordinary course of judicial proceedings has been interrupted by the rebellion. The source from which this military jurisdiction is to emanate is none other than the President of the United States, acting through the War Department and the Commissioner of the Freedmen's Bureau. The agents to carry out this military jurisdiction are to be selected either from the army or from civil life. The country is to be divided into districts and sub-districts, and the number of salaried agents to be employed may be equal to the number of counties or parishes in all the United States where freedmen and refugees are to be found. The subjects over which this military jurisdiction is to extend in every part of the United States, include protection to all employees, agents, and officers of this bureau in the exercise of the duties imposed upon them by the bill. In eleven States it is further to extend over all cases affecting freedmen and refugees discriminated against by local law, custom, or prejudice. In those eleven States the bill subjects any white person who may be charged with depriving a freedman of any civil rights or immunities belonging to white persons to imprisonment or fine, or both, without, however, defining the civil rights and immunities which are thus to be secured to the freedmen by military law. This military jurisdiction also extends to all questions that may arise respecting contracts. The agent, who is thus to exercise the office of a military judge, may be a stranger, entirely ignorant of the laws of the place, and exposed to the errors of judgment to which all men are liable. The exercise of power over which there is no legal supervision, by so vast a number of agents as is contemplated by the bill, must, by the very nature of man, be attended by acts of caprice, injustice, and passion. The trials having their origin under this bill are to take place without the intervention of a jury and without any fixed rules of law or evidence. The rules on which offences are to be heard and determined by the numerous agents, are such rules and regulations as the President, through the War Department, shall prescribe. No previous presentment is required, nor any indictment charging the commission of a crime against the laws ; but the trial must proceed on charges and specifications. The punishment will be not what the law declares, but such as a court-martial may think proper ; and from these arbitrary tribunals there lies no appeal, no writ of error to any of the courts in which the Constitution of the United States vests exclusively the judicial power of the country ; while the territory and the class of actions and offences that are made subject to this measure are so extensive, that the bill itself, should it become a law, will have no limitation in point of time, but will form a part of the permanent legislation of the country. I cannot reconcile a system of military jurisdiction of this kind with the words of the Constitution, which declare that 'no person shall be held to answer for a capital or otherwise infamous crime unless on a presentment or indictment of a grand jury, except in cases arising in the land or naval forces or in the militia when in actual service in time of war or public danger;' and that 'in all criminal prosecutions the accused shall enjoy the right to a speedy and public trial by an impartial jury of the State or district wherein the crime shall have been committed.'

"The safeguards which the wisdom and experience of ages taught our fathers to establish as securities for the protection of the innocent, the punishment of the guilty, and the equal administration of justice, are to be set aside, and for the sake of a more vigorous interposition in behalf of justice, we are to take the risk of the many acts of injustice that would of necessity follow from an almost countless number of agents established in every parish or county in nearly a third of the States of the Union, over whose decision there is to be no supervision or control by the Federal courts. The power that would be thus placed in the hands of the President, is such as in time of peace certainly ought never to be intrusted to any one man. If it be asked whether the creation of such a tribunal within a State is warranted as a measure of war, the question immediately presents itself, whether we are still engaged in war. Let us not unnecessarily disturb the commerce and credit and industry of the country, by declaring to the American people and the world that the United States are still in a condition of civil war. At present there is no part of our country in which the authority of the United States is disputed. Offences that may be committed by individuals should not work a forfeiture of the rights of the same communities. The country has entered or is returning to a state of peace and industry, and the rebellion is in fact at an end. The measure, therefore, seems to be as inconsistent with the actual condition of the country as it is at variance with the Constitution of the United States.

"If, passing from general considerations, we examine the bill in detail, it is open to weighty objections. In time of war it was eminently proper that we should provide for those who were passing suddenly from a condition of bondage to a state of freedom. But this bill proposes to make the Freedmen's Bureau, established by the act of 1865 as one of many great and extraordinary military measures to suppress a formidable rebellion, a permanent branch of the public administration, with its powers greatly enlarged. I have no reason to suppose, and I do not understand it to be alleged, that the act of March, 1865, has proved deficient for the purposes for which it was passed, although at that time, and for a considerable period thereafter, the Government of the United States remained unacknowledged in most of the States whose inhabitants had been involved in the rebellion. The institution of slavery, for the military destruction of which the Freedmen's Bureau was called into existence as an auxiliary force, has been already effectually and finally abrogated throughout the whole country by an amendment of the Constitution of the United States, and practically its eradication has received the assent and concurrence of most of those States in which it at any time had existed. I am not, therefore, able to discern in the country any thing to justify an apprehension that the powers and agencies of the Freedmen's Bureau, which were effective for the protection of freedmen and refugees during the actual continuation of hostilities and of African servitude, will now, in a time of peace and after the abolition of slavery, prove inadequate to the same proper ends. If I am correct in these views, there can be no necessity for the enlargement of the powers of the Bureau for which provision is made in the bill.

"The third section of the bill authorizes a general and unlimited grant of support to the destitute and suffering refugees and freedmen, and their wives and children. Succeeding sections make provision for the rent or purchase of landed estates for freedmen, and for the erection, for their benefit, of suitable asylums and schools, the expenses to be defrayed from the treasury of the whole people. The Congress of the United States has never, heretofore, thought itself competent to establish asylums beyond the limits of the District of Columbia, except for the benefit of our disabled soldiers and sailors. It has never founded schools for any class of our own people, not even for the orphans of those who have fallen in the defence of the Union, but has left the care of their education to the much more competent and efficient control of the States, of communities, of private associations, and of individuals. It has never deemed itself authorized to expend the public money for the rent or purchase of homes for the thousands, not to say millions, of the white race who are honestly toiling from day to day for their subsistence. A system for the support of indigent persons in the United States was never contemplated by the authors of the Constitution. Nor can any good reason be advanced why, as a permanent establishment, it should be founded for one class or color of our people more than for another.

Pending the war, many refugees and freedmen received support from the Government, but it was never intended that they should henceforth be fed, clothed, educated, and sheltered by the United States. The idea on which the slaves were assisted to freedom was, that on becoming free they would be a self-sustaining population. Any legislation that shall imply that they are not expected to attain a self-sustaining condition must have a tendency injurious alike to their character and their prosperity. The appointment of an agent for every county and parish will create an immense patronage, and the expense of the numerous officers and their clerks to be appointed by the President will be great in the beginning, with a tendency steadily to increase. The appropriations asked by the Freedmen's Bureau, as now established, for the year 1866, amount to $11,745,000. It may be safely estimated that the cost to be incurred under the pending bill will require double that amount,—more than the entire sum expended in any one year under the administration of the second Adams. If the presence of agents in every parish and county is to be considered as a war measure, opposition or even resistance might be provoked, so that to give effect to their jurisdiction troops would have to be stationed within reach of every one of them, and thus a standing army be rendered necessary. Large appropriations would therefore be required to sustain and enforce military jurisdiction in every county or parish from the Potomac to the Rio Grande. The condition of our fiscal affairs is encouraging; but, in order to sustain the present measure of public confidence, it is necessary that we practise not merely customary economy, but, as far as possible, severe retrenchment.

"In addition to the objections already stated, the fifth section of the bill proposes to take away land from its former owners, without any legal proceedings being first had, contrary to that provision of the Constitution which declares that no persons shall be deprived of life, liberty, or property without due process of law. It does not appear that a part of the lands which this section refers to may not be owned by minors or persons of unsound mind, or by those who have been faithful to all their obligations as citizens of the United States. If any portion of the land is held by such persons, it is not competent for any other authority to deprive them of it. If, on the other hand, it be found that the property is liable to confiscation, even then it cannot be appropriated to public purposes until, by due process of law, it shall have been declared forfeited to the Government.

"There are still further objections to the bill, on grounds seriously affecting the class of persons to whom it is designed to bring relief. It will tend to keep the mind of the freedman in a state of uncertain expectation and restlessness, while to those among whom he lives it will be a source of constant and vague apprehension. Undoubtedly the freedman should be protected by the civil authorities, especially by the exercise of all the constitutional powers of the courts of the United States and of the States. His condition is not so exposed as may at first be imagined. He is in a portion of the country where his labor cannot well be spared. Competition for his services from planters, from those who are constructing or repairing railroads, or from capitalists in his vicinage, or from other States, will enable him to command almost his own terms. He also possesses a perfect right to change his place of abode, and if, therefore, he does not find in one community or State a mode of life suited to his desires, or proper remuneration for his labor, he can move to another where labor is more esteemed and better rewarded. In truth, however, each State, induced by its own wants and interests, will do what is necessary and proper to retain within its borders all the labor that is needed for the development of its resources. The laws that regulate supply and demand will maintain their force, and the wages of the laborer will be regulated thereby. There is no danger that the great demand for labor will not operate in favor of the laborer. Neither is sufficient consideration given to the ability of the freedmen to protect and take care of themselves. It is no more than justice to them to believe that, as they have received their freedom with moderation and forbearance, so they will distinguish themselves by their industry and thrift, and soon show the world that in a condition of freedom they are self-sustaining and capable of selecting their own employment and their own places of abode ; of insisting for themselves on a proper remuneration, and of establishing and maintaining their own asylums and schools. It is earnestly hoped that instead of wasting away, they will, by their own efforts, establish for themselves a condition of respectability and prosperity. It is certain that they can attain to that condition only through their own merits and exertions. In this connection the query presents itself, whether the system proposed by the bill will not, when put into complete operation, practically transfer the entire care, support, and control of four millions of emancipated slaves to agents, overseers, or taskmasters, who, appointed at Washington, are to be located in every county and parish throughout the United States containing freedmen and refugees. Such a system would inevitably tend to such a concentration of power in the Executive as would enable him, if so disposed, to control the action of a numerous class, and use them for the attainment of his own political ends.

"I cannot but add another very grave objection to this bill. The Constitution imperatively declares, in connection with taxation, that each State shall have at least one representative, and fixes the rule for the number to which in future times each State shall be entitled. It also provides that the Senate of the United States shall be composed of two senators from each State, and adds with peculiar force that no State, without its consent, shall be deprived of its equal suffrage in the Senate. The original act was necessarily passed in the absence of the States chiefly to be affected, because their people were then contumaciously engaged in the rebellion. Now the case is changed, and some, at least, of the States are attending Congress by loyal representatives, soliciting the allowance of the constitutional right of representation. At the time, however, of the consideration and the passing of the bill there was no senator or representative in Congress from the eleven States which are to be mainly affected by its provisions. The very fact that reports were and are made against the good disposition of the country, is an additional reason why they need and should have representatives of their own in Congress to explain their condition, reply to accusations, and assist by their local knowledge in the perfecting of measures immediately affecting themselves; while the liberty of deliberation would then be free, and Congress would have full power to decide according to its judgment. There could be no objection urged that the States most interested had not been permitted to be heard. The principle is firmly fixed in the minds of the American people that there should be no taxation without representation. Great burdens are now to be borne by all the country, and we may best demand that they shall be borne without murmur when they are voted by a majority of representatives of all the people.

"I would not interfere with the unquestionable right of Congress to judge, each House for itself, of the elections, returns, and qualifications of its own members. But that authority cannot be construed as including the right to shut out in time of peace any State from representation to which it is entitled by the Constitution. At present all the people of eleven States are excluded,—those who were most faithful during the war not less than others. The State of Tennessee, for instance, whose authorities engaged in rebellion, was restored to all her constitutional relations to the Union by the patriotism and energy of her injured and betrayed people. Before the war was brought to a termination they had placed themselves in relations with the General Government, had established a State government of their own, and, as they were not included in the emancipation proclamation, they, by their own act, had amended their constitution so as to abolish slavery within the limits of their State. I know no reason why the State of Tennessee, for example, should not fully enjoy all her constitutional relations to the United States.

"The President of the United States stands towards the country in a somewhat different attitude from that of any member of Congress chosen from a single district or State. The President is chosen by the people of all the States. Eleven States are not, at this time, represented in either branch of Congress. It would seem to be his duty on all proper occasions to present their just claims to Congress. There always will be differences of opinion in the community, and individuals may be guilty of transgressions of the law. But these do not constitnte valid objections against the right of a State to representation. I would in no wise interfere with the discretion of Congress with regard to the qualifications of members; but I hold it my duty to recommend to you in the interests of peace, and in the interests of the Union, the admission of every State to its share of public legislation, when, however insubordinate, insurgent, or rebellious its people may have been, it presents itself not only in an attitude of loyalty and harmony, but in the persons of their representatives whose loyalty cannot be doubted under existing constitutional or legal tests. It is plain that an indefinite or permanent exclusion of any part of the country from representation must be attended by a spirit of disquiet and complaint. It is unwise and dangerous to pursue a course of measures which will unite any large section of the country against another section of the country, no matter how much the latter may predominate. The course of immigration, the development of industry and business, and natural causes will raise up at the South men as devoted to the Union as those of any other part of the land. But if they are all excluded from Congress, if in a permanent statute they are declared not to be in full constitutional relations to the country, they may think they have cause to become a unit in feelings and sentiments against the Government. Under the political education of the American people, the idea is inherent and ineradicable that the consent of the majority of the whole people is necessary to secure a willing acquiescence in legislation. The bill under consideration refers to certain of the States as though they had not 'been fully restored in all their constitutional relations to the United States.' If they have not, let us at once act together to secure that desirable end at the earliest possible moment. It is hardly necessary for me to inform Congress that, in my own judgment, most of those States, so far at least as depends upon their own action, have already been fully restored, and are to be deemed to be entitled to enjoy their constitutional rights as members of the Union. Reasoning from the Constitution itself, and from the actual situation of the country, I feel not only entitled, but bound, to assume that with the Federal courts restored in the several States, and in the full exercise of their functions, the rights and interests of all classes of the people will, with the aid of the military in cases of resistance to the law, be essentially protected against unconstitutional infringement and violation. Should this expectation unhappily fail, which I do not anticipate, then the Executive is already armed with the powers conferred by the act of March, 1865, establishing the Freedmen's Bureau; and hereafter, as heretofore, he can employ the land and naval forces of the country to suppress insurrection and to overcome obstructions to the laws.

"I return the bill to the Senate in the earnest hope that a measure involving questions and interests so important to the country will not become a law, unless upon deliberate consideration by the people it shall receive the sanction of an enlightened public judgment.

"ANDREW JOHNSON.

"WASHINGTON, D. C., *Feb.* 19, 1866."

CHAPTER XVI.

SPEECH TO THE CITIZENS OF WASHINGTON, FEB. 22D, 1866.

On Washington's birthday a meeting was held in Washington to indorse the action of the President in vetoing the Freedmen's Bureau Bill. All the prominent men in the city joined in it, and the crowd was immense. After the conclusion of the meeting, a committee appointed for the purpose waited upon the President to present him the resolutions, when he appeared and made the following speech to the assembled multitude:

"Fellow-Citizens—for I presume I have the right to address you as such—to the committee who have conducted and organized this meeting so far, I have to render my sincere thanks for the compliments and approbation they have manifested in their personal address to myself, and in the resolutions they have adopted. Fellow-citizens—I was about to tender my thanks to the committee who waited upon me and presented me with the resolutions adopted on this occasion—resolutions, as I understand, complimentary to the policy pursued by this administration since it came into power. I am free to say to you on this occasion, that it is extremely gratifying to me to know that so large a portion of my fellow-citizens approve and indorse the policy that has been adopted, and *is intended to be carried out.* (Applause.) That policy has been one which was intended to restore the glorious union of these States and their original relations to the government of the United States. (Prolonged applause.) This seems to be a day peculiarly appropriate for such a manifestation—the day that gave birth to him who founded this Government—the Father of his Country; of him who stood at the head of the government when all the States entered into the Union. This day, I say, is peculiarly appropriate to indorse the restoration of the Union of these States founded by the Father of his Country. Washington, whose name this city bears, is embalmed in the hearts of all who love free government. (A voice—"So is Andrew Johnson.") Washington, who, in the language of his eulogists, was "First in peace, first in war, first in the hearts of his countrymen." No people can claim him; no nation can appropriate him; his reputation and life are the common inheritance of all who love free government.

THE PRESIDENT'S MOTTO THAT OF ANDREW JACKSON.

"I to-day had the pleasure of attending the National Washington Monument Association, which is directing its efforts to complete the monument erected to his memory. I was glad to meet them, and, so far as I could, to give them my humble influence. A monument is being erected to him within a stone's throw of the spot from which I address you. Let it be completed. (Cheers.) Let the pledges which all these

States, associations, and corporations have placed in that monument of their faith and love for this Union be preserved. Let it be completed, and in this connection let me refer to the motto upon the stone sent from my own State. God bless (A voice—"And bless you") a State which has struggled for the preservation of the Union, in the field and in the councils of the nation, and is now struggling in consequence of the interruption that has taken place in her relations with the Federal Government, growing out of the rebellion, but struggling to recover those relations and take her stand where she has stood since 1796. A motto is inscribed on that stone sent here to be placed in that monument of freedom and in commemoration of Washington. I stand by that sentiment, and she is willing to stand by it. It was the sentiment enunciated by the immortal Andrew Jackson, 'The Federal Union—it must be preserved.' (Wild shouts of applause.) Were it possible to have the great man whose statue is now before me, and whose portrait is behind me in the Capitol, and whose sentiment is inscribed on the stone deposited in the monument—were it possible to communicate with the illustrious dead, and he could be informed of or made to understand the working or progress of faction, rebellion, and treason, the bones of the old man would stir in their coffin, and he would rise and shake off the habiliments of the tomb ; he would extend that long arm and finger of his, and he would reiterate that glorious sentiment, 'The Federal Union—it must be preserved.' (Applause.) But we see and witness what has transpired since his day. We remember what he did in 1833, when treason, treachery, and infidelity to the

Government and Constitution of the United States then stalked forth. It was his power and influence that then crushed the treason in its infancy. It was then stopped : but only for a time—the spirit continued. There were men disaffected to the Government both North and South. We had peculiar institutions, of which some complained and to which others were attached. One portion of our countrymen advocated that institution in the South ; another opposed it in the North ; and it resulted in creating two extremes. The one in the South reached the point at which they were prepared to dissolve the Government of the United States, to secure and preserve their peculiar institution ; and in what I may say on this occasion I want to be understood."

THE REPUBLICANS AS DISUNIONISTS.

"There was another portion of our countrymen who were opposed to this peculiar institution in the South, and who went to the extreme of being willing to break up the Government to get clear of it. [Applause.] I am talking to you to-day in the common phrase, and assume to be nothing but a citizen, and one who has been fighting for the Constitution and to preserve the Government. These two parties have been arrayed against each other ; and I stand before you to-day, as I did in the Senate in 1860, in the presence of those who were making war on the Constitution, and who wanted to disrupt the Government, to denounce, as I then did in my place, those who were so engaged, as traitors. I have never ceased to repeat, and so far as my efforts could go, to carry out, the sentiments I then uttered. [Cheers.] I have already remarked that there were two parties, one for destroying the Government to preserve slavery, and the other to break up the Government to destroy slavery. The objects to be accomplished were different, it is true, so far as slavery is concerned, but they agreed in one thing, and that was the breaking up of the Government. They agreed in the destruction of the Government, the precise thing which I have stood up to oppose. *Whether the disunionists come from the South or the North I stand now where I did then,* to vindicate the Union of these States and the Constitution of the country." [Applause.]

THE DOORS OPEN TO THE SOUTH.

"The rebellion or treason manifested itself in the South. I stood by the Government. I said I was for the Union with slavery, or I was for the Union without slavery. In either alternative, I was for my Government and the Constitution. [Applause.] The Government has stretched forth its strong arm, and with its physical power has put down treason in the field. Yes, the *section* of country which has arrayed itself against the Government has been put down by the Government itself. Now, what do these people say? We said, 'No compromise; we can settle this question with the South in eight and forty hours.' How? 'Disband your armies, acknowledge the Constitution of the United States, obey the law, and the whole question is settled.' Well, their armies have been disbanded. They come forward now in a spirit of magnanimity and say, 'We were mistaken; we made an effort to carry out the doctrine of secession and dissolve the Union, but we have failed; and, having traced this thing to a logical and physical consequence and result, we now again come forward and acknowledge the flag of our country, obedient to the Constitution and the supremacy of the law.' [Cheers.] I say, then, when you have yielded to the law, when you acknowledge your allegiance to the Government, *I am ready to open the doors of the Union and restore you to your old relations to the Government of our fathers.*" [Prolonged applause.]

THE EXECUTIVE POWER.

"Who, I ask, has suffered more for the Union than I have? I shall not now repeat the wrongs or suffering inflicted upon me; but it is not the way to deal with a whole people in the spirit of revenge. I know much has been said about the exercise of the pardoning power, so far as the Executive power is concerned. There is no one who has labored harder than I have to have the principal conscious and intelligent traitors brought to justice; to have the law vindicated, and the great fact vindicated that treason is a crime. Yet, while conscious, intelligent traitors are to be punished, should whole States, communities, and people be made to submit to and bear the penalty of death? I have, perhaps, as much hostility and as much resentment as a man ought to have; but we should conform our action and our conduct to the example of Him who founded our holy religion—not that I would liken this to it or bring any comparison, for I am not going to detain you long."

THE CONDITION OF AFFAIRS, AND HOW IT IS TO BE REMEDIED.

"But, gentlemen, I came into power under the Constitution of the country and by the approbation of the people. And what did I find? I found eight millions of people who were in fact condemned under the law—and the penalty was death. Under the idea of revenge and resentment, they were to be annihilated and destroyed. Oh, how different this from the example set by the holy Founder of our religion, whose divine arm touches the horizon and embraces the whole earth! Yes, He who founded this great scheme came into the world and found our race condemned under the law—and the sentence was death. What was His example? Instead of putting the world or a nation to death, He went forth with grace and attested by His blood and His wounds that He would die and let the nation live. [Applause.] Let them become loyal and willing supporters and defenders of our glorious Stripes and Stars and the Constitution of our country. *Let their leaders, the conscious, intelligent traitors, suffer the penalty of the law*, but for the great mass who have been forced into this rebellion and misled by their leaders, I say *leniency, kindness, trust, and confidence*." [Enthusiastic cheers.]

THE RADICAL REBELS.

"But, my countrymen, after having passed through the rebellion and given such evidence as I have—though men croak a great deal about it now—(laughter) when I look back through the battle-fields and see many of those brave men, in whose company I was in part of the rebellion where it was most difficult and doubtful to be found; before the smoke of battle has scarcely passed away; before the blood shed has scarcely congealed, what do we find? The rebellion is put down by the strong arm of the Government in the field; *but is it the only way in which we can have rebellion?* They struggled for the breaking up of the Government, but before they are scarcely out of the battle-field, and before our brave men have scarcely returned to their homes to renew the ties of affection and love, we find ourselves almost *in the midst of another rebellion.* [Applause.] The war to suppress our rebellion was to prevent the separation of the States, and thereby change the character of the Government and weakening its power. Now, what is the change? There is an attempt to concentrate the power of the Government in the hands of a few, and *thereby bring about a consolidation, which is equally dangerous and objectionable with separation.* [Enthusiastic applause.] We find that powers are assumed and attempted to be exercised of a most extraordinary character. What are they? We find that *Government can be revolutionized, can be changed without going into the battle-field.* Sometimes revolutions the most disastrous to the people are effected without shedding blood. The substance of our Government may be taken away, leaving only the form and shadow. Now, what are the attempts? What is being proposed?

USURPATIONS OF CONGRESS.

"We find that, in fact, by an irresponsible central directory, nearly all the powers of Government are assumed without even consulting the legislative or executive departments of the Government. Yes, and by resolution reported by a committee upon whom all the legislative power of the Government has been conferred, that principle in the Constitution which authorizes and empowers each branch of the legislative department to be judges of the election and qualifications of its own members, has been virtually taken away from those departments and conferred upon a committee, who must report before they can act under the Constitution and allow members duly elected to take their seats. By this rule they assume that there must be laws passed; that there must be recognition in respect to a State in the Union, with all its practical relations restored, before the respective houses of Congress, under the Constitution, shall judge of the election and qualifications of its own members. What position is that? You have been struggling for four years to put down the rebellion. You denied in the beginning of the struggle that any State had the right to go out. You said that they had neither the right nor the power. The issue has been made, and it has been settled that a State has neither the right nor the power to go out of the Union. And when you have settled that by the executive and military power of the Government, and by the public judgment, you *turn around and assume that they are out and shall not come in.*" [Laughter and cheers.]

NOT THE PRESIDENT'S POSITION.

"I am free to say to you, as your Executive, that *I am not prepared to take any such position.* I said in the Senate, at the very inception of the rebellion, that States had no right to go out and that they had no power to go out. That question has been settled. And I cannot turn round now and give the direct lie to all I profess to have done in the last five years

[Laughter and applause.] I can do no such thing. I say that when these States comply with the Constitution, when they have given sufficient evidence of their loyalty, and that they can be trusted, when they yield obedience to the law, I say, *extend to them the right hand of fellowship*, and let peace and union be restored. [Loud cheers.] I have fought traitors and treason in the South; I opposed the Davises and Toombses, the Slidells, and a long list of others whose names I need not repeat; and now, when I turn round at the other end of the line, I find men—I care not by what name you call them—[A voice, 'Call them traitors'], who still stand opposed to the restoration of the Union of these States. And I am free to say to you that I am still for the preservation of this compact; I am still for the restoration of this Union; I am still in favor of this great Government of ours going on and following out its destiny. [A voice, 'Give us the names.']"

THE DISUNIONISTS ANNOUNCED BY NAME.

"A gentleman calls for their names. Well, suppose I should give them. [A voice, 'We know them.'] I look upon them—I repeat it, as President or citizen—as being as much opposed to the fundamental principles of this Government, and believe they are as much laboring to pervert or destroy them as were the men who fought against us. [A voice, 'What are the names?'] *I say Thaddeus Stevens, of Pennsylvania*—[tremendous applause]—*I say Charles Sumner*—[great applause]—*I say Wendell Phillips, and others of the same stripe, are among them.* [A voice, 'Give it to Forney.'] Some gentleman in the crowd says,

'Give it to Forney.' I have only just to say that *I do not waste my ammunition upon dead ducks.*" [Laughter and applause.]

THE PRESIDENT FOR THE WHOLE COUNTRY.

"I stand for my country, I stand for the Constitution, where I placed my feet from my entrance into public life. They may traduce me, they may slander me, they may vituperate; but let me say to you that it has no effect upon me. [Cheers.] And let me say in addition, that *I do not intend to be bullied by my enemies.* [Applause, and a cry, 'The people will sustain you.'] I know, my countrymen, that it has been insinuated, and not only insinuated, but said directly—the intimation has been given in high places—that if such a usurpation of power had been exercised two hundred years ago in a particular reign it would have cost a certain individual his head. What usurpation has Andrew Johnson been guilty of? ['None, none.'] The usurpation I have been guilty of has always been standing between the people and the encroachments of power. And because I dared to say in a conversation with a fellow-citizen, and a senator too, that I thought amendments to the Constitution ought not to be so frequent; that their effect would be that it would lose all its dignity; that the old instrument would be lost sight of in a short time; because I happened to say that if it was amended such and such amendments should be adopted—it was a usurpation of power that would have cost a king his head at a certain time. [Laughter and applause.] And in connection with this subject it was explained by the same gentleman that we were in the midst of an earthquake, that he trembled and could not yield. [Laughter.] Yes, *there is an earthquake coming. There is a ground-swell coming of popular judgment and indignation.* ['That's true.'] The American people will speak by their interests, and they will know who are their friends and who their enemies. What positions have I held under this government? Beginning with an alderman and running through all branches of the Legislature. [A voice—'From a tailor up.') Some gentleman says I have been a tailor. [Tremendous applause.] Now, that did not discomfit me in the least; for when I used to be a tailor I had the reputation of being a good one, and making close fits—[great laughter]—always punctual with my customers, and always did good work. [A voice—'No patchwork.'] No, I do not want any patchwork. I want a whole suit. But I will pass by this little facetiousness. My friends may say you are President, and you must not talk about such things. When principles are involved, my countrymen, when the existence of my country is imperilled, I will act as I did on former occasions, and speak what I think. I was saying that I had held nearly all positions, from alderman, through both branches of Congress, to that which I now occupy, and who is there that will say that Andrew Johnson ever made a pledge that he did not redeem, or made a promise he did not fulfil? Who will say that he has ever acted otherwise than in fidelity to the great mass of the American people? They may talk about beheading and usurpation; but when I am beheaded I want the American people to witness I do not want by inuendoes, by indirect marks in high places, to see the man who has assassination brooding in his bosom, exclaim, 'This presidential obstacle must be gotten out of the way.' I make use of a very strong expression when I say that I have no doubt the *intention was to incite assassination*, and so get out of the way the obstacle from place and power. Whether by assassination or not, there are individuals in this Government, I doubt not, who want to destroy our institutions and change the character of the Government. Are they not satisfied with the blood which has been shed? Does not the murder of Lincoln appease the vengeance and wrath of the opponents of this Government? Are they still unslaked? Do they still want more blood? Have they not got honor and courage enough to attain their object otherwise than by the hands of the assassin? No, no; I am not afraid of assassins attacking me where a brave and courageous man would attack another. I only dread him when he would go in disguise, his footsteps noiseless. If it is blood they want, let them have courage enough to strike like men. I know they are willing to wound, but they are afraid to strike. [Applause.] If my blood is to be shed because I vindicate the Union and the preservation of this Government in its original purity and character, let it be shed; let an altar to the Union be erected, and then, if it is necessary, take me and lay me upon it, and the blood that now warms and animates my existence shall be poured out as a fit libation to the Union of these States. [Great applause.] But let the opponents of this Government remember that when it is poured out, 'the blood of the martyrs will be the seed of the Church.' [Cheers.] Gentlemen, this Union will grow—it will continue to increase in strength and power, though it may be cemented and cleansed in blood. I have talked longer now than I intended. Let me thank you for the honor you have done me."

MR. LINCOLN'S IDEA OF COMPULSORY REPRESENTATION.

"So far as this Government is concerned, let me say one word in reference to the amendments to the Constitution of the United States. When I reached Washington for the purpose of being inaugurated as Vice-President of the United States I had a conversation with Mr. Lincoln. We were talking about the condition of affairs and in reference to matters in my own State. I said that we had called a convention, had amended our Constitution by abolishing slavery in the State—a State not embraced in his proclamation. All this met his approbation and gave him encouragement, and in talking upon the amendment to the Constitution, he said: 'When the amendment to the Constitution is adopted by three-fourths of the States, we shall have all, or pretty nearly all. I am in favor of amending the Constitution, if there was one other adopted.' Said I, 'What is that, Mr. President?' Said he, 'I have labored to preserve this Union. I have toiled four years; I have been subjected to calumny and misrepresentation, yet my great desire has been to preserve the Union of these States intact under the Constitution as they were before.' 'But,' said I, 'Mr. President, what amendment do you refer to?' He said he thought there should be an amendment to the Constitution which would compel all the States to send their Senators and Representatives to the Congress of the United States. Yes, compel them. The idea was in his mind that it was a part of the doctrine of secession to break up the Government by States withdrawing their Senators and Representatives from Congress; and, therefore, he desired a Constitutional amendment to compel them to be sent."

THE DISUNION IDEA OF NO REPRESENTATION.

"How now does the matter stand? In the Constitution of the country, even that portion of it which provides for the amendment of the organic law, says that no State shall, without its consent, be deprived of its representation in the Senate. And now what do we find? We find the position taken that States shall not be represented; that we may impose taxes; that we may send our tax-gatherers to every region and portion of a State; that the people are to be oppressed with taxes; but when they come here to participate in legislation of the country, they are met at the door, and told, 'No! you must pay your taxes; you must bear the burdens of the Government; but you must not participate in the legislation of the country, which is to affect you for all time.' Is this just? ['No, no.'] Then, I say, let us admit into the councils of the nation those who are unmistakably and unequivocally loyal—those men who acknowledge their allegiance to the Government and swear to support the Constitution. It is all embraced in that. The amplification of an oath makes no difference, if a man is not loyal. But you may adopt whatever test oath you please to prove their loyalty. That is a matter of detail for which I care nothing. Let him be unquestionably loyal, owing his allegiance to the Government and willing to support it in its hour of peril and of need, and I am willing to trust him. I know that some do not attach so much importance to this principle as I do. But one principle we carried through. The Revolution was fought that there should be no taxation without representation. I hold to that principle, laid down as fundamental by our fathers. If it was good then, it is now. If it was a rule to stand by then, it is a rule to stand by now. It is a fundamental principle that should be adhered to as long as governments last."

THE CONSTITUTION OUR GUIDE AND SAFETY.

"I know it was said by some during the rebellion that our Constitution had been rolled up as a piece of parchment and laid away ; that in the time of war and rebellion there was no Constitution. Well, we know that sometimes, from the very great necessity of the case, from a great emergency, we must do unconstitutional things in order to preserve the Constitution itself. But if, while the rebellion was going on, the Constitution was rolled up as a piece of parchment ; if it was violated in some particular to save the Government, there may have been some excuse to justify it : but now that peace has come, now the war is over, we want a written Constitution, and I say the time has come to take the Constitution down, unroll it, read it, and understand its provisions. Now, if you have saved the Government by violating the Constitution in war, you can only save it in peace by preserving the Constitution of our fathers as it is now unfolded. It must now be read and understood by the American people. I come here to-day, as far as I can in making these remarks, to vindicate the Constitution and to save it, for it does seem to me that encroachment after encroachment is proposed. I stand to-day prepared, as far as I can, to resist these encroachments upon the Constitution and Government. Now that we have peace, let us enforce the Constitution; let us live under and by its provisions; let it be published; let it be printed in blazing characters, as if it were in the heavens, punctuated with stars, that all may read and understand; let us consult that instrument; let us digest its provisions, understand them, and, understanding, abide by them. I tell the opponents of the Government, I care not from what quarter they come—whether from the East, West, North, or South, you who are *engaged in the work of breaking up the Government by amendments to the Constitution*, that the principles of free government, all deeply rooted in the American heart, all the powers combined, I care not of what character they are, *cannot destroy that great instrument*, that great chart of freedom. They may seem to succeed for a time; but their attempts will be futile. They might as well undertake to lock up the winds or chain the waves of the ocean and confine them to limits. They may think now it can be done by a concurrent resolution; but when it is submitted to the popular judgment and to the popular will, they will find that they *might as well introduce a resolution to repeal the laws of gravity as to keep this Union from being restored.* It is just about as feasible to resist the great law of gravity, which binds all to a common centre, as that great law which will bring back these States to their regular relations with the Union. All these conspiracies and machinations, North and South, I cannot prevent. All that is wanted is time, until the American people can get to see what is going on. I would the whole American people could be assembled here to-day, as you are. I wish we had an amphitheatre capacious enough to hold these thirty millions of people, that they could be here and witness the struggle that is going on to preserve the Constitution of their fathers. They would settle this question. They could see who it is, and how and what kind of spirit is breaking up this free Government. Yes, when they come to see the struggle and understand who is for and who against them, if you could make them perform the part of gladiators, in the first tilt you would find the enemies of the country crushed and helpless."

ANDY JOHNSON'S LUCK.

"I have detained you longer than I intended. [Voices, 'Go on.'] We are in a great struggle. I am your instrument. Who is there I have not toiled and labored for? Where is the man or woman, either in public or private life, who has not always received my attention or my time? Pardon the egotism. They say that man Johnson is a lucky man, that no man can defeat me. I will tell you what constitutes luck. It is due to right, and being for the people; that is what constitutes good luck. Somehow or other the people will find out and understand who is for and who is against them. I have been placed in as many trying positions as any mortal man was ever placed in, but so far I have not deserted the people, and I believe they will not desert me. What principle have I violated? What sentiments have I swerved from? Can they put their finger upon it? Have you heard of them pointing out any discrepancy? Have you heard them quote my predecessor, who fell a martyr to his country's cause, as going in opposition or in contradistinction to any thing that I have done? The very policy which I am pursuing now was pursued under his administration—was being pursued by him when that inscrutable Providence saw fit to summon him, I trust, to a better world. Where is there one principle adopted by him in reference to this restoration that I have departed from. ['None, none.'] The war, then, is not simply upon me, but upon my predecessor. I have tried to do my duty. I know that some people, in their jealousy, have made the remark that the White House is President. Just let me say that the charms of the White House and all that sort of flummery has less influence with me than with those who are talking about it. The little I eat or wear does not amount to much. That required to sustain me and my little family is very little, for I am not feeding many, though in one sense of consanguinity I am akin to everybody. The conscious satisfaction of having performed my duty to my country is all the reward I have."

STAND BY THE CONSTITUTION.

"Then, in conclusion, let me ask this vast concourse, this sea of upturned faces, to join with me in standing round the Constitution of our country. It is again unfolded and the people are invited to read, to understand, and to maintain its provisions. Let us stand by the Constitution of our fathers, though the heavens themselves may fall. Let us stand by it, though faction may rage. Though taunts and jeers may come, though vituperation may come in its most violent character, *I will be found standing by the Constitution as the chief rock of our safety*, as the palladium of our civil and religious liberty. Yes, let us cling to it as the mariner clings to his last plank when night and tempest close around him. Accept my thanks for the indulgence you have given me in making the extemporaneous remarks I have upon this occasion. Let us go forward, forgetting the past and looking to the future, and try to restore our country. Trusting in Him who rules on high that ere long our Union will be restored, and that we will have peace, not only on earth, but especially with the people of the United States, and good-will, I thank you, my countrymen, for the spirit you have manifested on this occasion. When your country is gone, and you are about, look out and you will find the humble individual who now stands before you weeping over its final dissolution."

A New York paper refers to the reception of the above remarkable speech of President Johnson in Europe in the following terms :

"The English papers praise in the strongest terms the President's speech delivered on Washington's birthday. That speech has put before the world the true, clear view of the state of parties here, and has extorted, for the leader of the people, expressions of the most earnest admiration from quarters hitherto content to cavil and sneer at all that originates on this side the Atlantic. The speech that the radicals denounced as horrible, vulgar, unfortunate, and outrageous ; that some of the President's friends even were inclined to excuse and explain, and that the Herald declared to be greater and finer than any thing in Demosthenes, receives from Europe the highest possible meed of praise for its energetic simplicity, and for its sentiments is declared to be 'not unworthy the great founder of the American republic.' Such a speech, says the London Times, 'has not often been heard in America—a speech entirely free from tawdry ornament or ambitious metaphor, but conveying the firmest determination and the most enlightened principles in the plainest and simplest language.' And the same paper says in another article: 'There is a stamp of reality and proud self-confidence in this appeal to the sovereign people, which obliterates the effect of some indiscreet expressions, and makes us feel that Mr. Johnson is equal to guiding the destinies of a great nation through a perilous crisis. * * * No hereditary monarch, nor even an elective emperor, inheriting the traditions and administrative system of an hereditary monarchy, can ever be placed in the same position as President Johnson, and it is to be feared that few princes born in the purple would be capable of facing a great emergency with equal courage and dignity.' Mr. Johnson, it is said, 'if any man ever did, occupies nobly and worthily a great historic position. The destinies of millions of the human race depend upon him, and he rises fully to the height of the occasion. Men whose nerves are shaken by the holiday politics of such a country as ours will stand aghast at the audacity with which President Johnson confronts his adversaries.' Such is the European verdict, and the country may thus see that, viewed from a proper distance—a distance that enables one to take in its full proportions and relations to the state of the country—the President's speech is not less great and statesman-like than we declared it to be from the first."

CHAPTER XVII.

THE CIVIL RIGHTS BILL.—THE PRESIDENT'S VETO.

THE veto by President Johnson of the "Civil Rights Bill," is generally acknowledged as one of the ablest state papers ever emanating from the Executive Department. It shows that Mr. Johnson has a mind at once logical and capable of a complete comprehension of any subject before him. The veto is unanswerable, and though Senator Trumbull, of Illinois, undertook a reply to it, he utterly failed in demolishing it, and only succeeded in advertising the inconsistency of his own political opinion. "There," said a Radical to a Johnson man, "read Mr. Trumbull's speech" (handing him a copy), "and see how completely Mr. Johnson is answered." "Yes," replied the Johnson man, "if Mr. Trumbull has answered Mr. Johnson, he has also demolished himself, for I have an extract from a speech delivered by Mr. T. in the Senate, on the 12th of December, 1859, in which I find this language:

"'In my judgment, there is a distinction between the white and black races, made by Omnipotence itself. I do not believe these two races can live happily or pleasantly together.'"

This extract silenced his Radical friend, if it did not convince him that Mr. Trumbull was like the lawyer, that he is trying to make the worse appear the better reason. Mr. Johnson's veto is so able and statesmanlike a letter that I make no apology in presenting it to my readers in full. The following is the message:

To the Senate of the United States:

I regret that the bill which has passed both Houses of Congress, entitled "An Act to protect all persons in the United States in their civil rights, and furnish the means of their vindication," contains provisions which I cannot approve, consistently with my sense of duty to the whole people, and my obligations to the Constitution of the United States. I am, therefore, constrained to return it to the Senate (the House in which it originated) with my objections to its becoming a law.

By the first section of the bill, all persons born in the United States, and not subject to any foreign power, excluding Indians not taxed, are declared to be citizens of the United States. This provision comprehends the Chinese of the Pacific States, Indians subject to taxation, the people called Gipsies, as well as the entire race designated as blacks, people of color, negroes, mulattoes, and persons of African blood. Every individual of these races, born in the United States, is by the bill made a citizen of the United States. It does not purport to declare or confer any other right of citizenship than Federal citizenship; it does not propose to give these classes of persons any status as citizens of States, except that which may result from their status as citizens of the United States. The power to confer the right of State citizenship is just as exclusively with the several States, as the power to confer the right of Federal citizenship is with Congress. The right of Federal citizenship, thus to be conferred in the several excepted ratios before mentioned, is now, for the first time, proposed to be given by law. If, as is claimed by many, all persons who are native born, already are, by virtue of the Constitution, citizens of the United States, the passage of the pending bill cannot be necessary to make them such. If, on the other hand, such persons are not citizens, as may be assumed from the proposed legislation to make them such, the grave question presents itself whether, where eleven of the thirty-six States are unrepresented in Congress at the time, it is sound policy to make our entire colored population, and all other excepted classes, citizens of the United States. Four millions of them have just emerged from slavery into freedom. Can it be reasonably supposed that they possess the requisite qualifications to entitle them to all the privileges and immunities of citizenship of the United States? Have the people of the several States expressed such a conviction? It may also be asked, whether it is necessary that they should be declared citizens in order that they may be secured in the enjoyment of the civil rights proposed to be conferred by the bill? Those rights are, by Federal as well as by State laws, secured to all domiciled aliens and foreigners, even before the completion of the process of naturalization; and it may safely be assumed that the same enactments are sufficient to give like protection and benefits to those for whom this bill provides special legislation. Besides, the policy of the Government, from its origin to the present time, seems to have been that persons who are strangers to and unfamiliar with our institutions and our laws, should pass through a certain probation; at the end of which, before attaining the coveted prize, they must give evidence of their fitness to receive and to exercise the rights of citizens as contemplated by the Constitution of the United States. The bill in effect proposes a discrimination against large numbers of intelligent, worthy and patriotic foreigners, and in favor of the negro, to whom, after long years of bondage, the avenues to freedom and intelligence have just now been suddenly opened. He must of necessity, from his previous unfortunate condition of servitude, be less informed as to the nature and character of our institutions than he who, coming from abroad, has to some extent, at least, familiarized himself with the principles of a Government to which he voluntarily intrusts life, liberty, and the pursuit of happiness. Yet it is now proposed by a single legislative enactment to confer the rights of citizens upon all persons of African descent, born within the extended limits of the United States, while persons of foreign birth, who make our land their home, must undergo a probation of five years, and can only then become citizens upon proof that they are of good moral character, attached to the principles of the Constitution of the United States, and well disposed to the good order and happiness of the same. The first section of the bill also contains an enumeration of the rights to be enjoyed by those classes so made citizens in every State and

Territory of the United States. These rights are, to make and enforce contracts, to sue, be parties and give evidence, to inherit, purchase, lease, sell, hold, or convey real and personal property, and to have full and equal benefit of all laws and proceedings for the security of persons and property as is enjoyed by white citizens. So, too, they are made subject to the same punishments, pains, and penalties common with white citizens, and to none others. Thus a perfect equality of the white and colored races is attempted to be fixed by a Federal law in every State of the Union, over the vast field of State jurisdiction covered by these enumerated rights. In no one of them can any State exercise any power of discrimination between different races. In the exercise of State policy over matters exclusively affecting the people of each State, it has frequently been thought expedient to discriminate between the two races. By the statutes of some of the States, North as well as South, it is enacted, for instance, that no white person shall intermarry with a negro or mulatto. Chancellor Kent says, speaking of the blacks, that marriages between them and the whites are forbidden in some of the States where slavery does not exist, and they are prohibited in all the slaveholding States by law; and when not absolutely contrary to law, they are revolting, and regarded as an offence against public decorum. I do not say that this bill repeals State laws, on the subject of marriage between the two races, for as the whites are forbidden to intermarry with the blacks, the blacks can only make such contracts as the whites themselves are allowed to make, and therefore cannot, under this bill, enter into the marriage contract with the whites. I take this discrimination, however, as an instance of the State policy as to discrimination, and to inquire whether, if Congress can abrogate all State laws of discrimination between the two races, in the matter of real estate, of suits, and of contracts generally, Congress may not also repeal the State laws as to the contract of marriage between the races? Hitherto, every subject embraced in the enumeration of rights contained in the bill has been considered as exclusively belonging to the States; they all relate to the internal policy and economy of the respective States. They are matters which, in each State, concern the domestic condition of its people, varying in each according to its peculiar circumstances and the safety and well-being of its own citizens. I do not mean to say that upon all these subjects there are not Federal restraints; as, for instance, in the State power of legislation over contracts, there is a Federal limitation that no State shall pass a law impairing the obligations of contracts; and, as to crimes, that no State shall pass an *ex-post-facto* law; and, as to money, that no State shall make any thing but gold and silver a legal tender. But where can we find a Federal prohibition against the power of any State to discriminate, as do most of them, between aliens and citizens, between artificial persons called corporations, and naturalized persons, in the right to hold real estate? If it be granted that Congress can repeal all State laws discriminating between whites and blacks, in the subjects covered by this bill, why, it may be asked, may not Congress repeal, in the same way, all State laws discriminating between the two races on the subject of suffrage and office? If Congress shall declare by law who shall hold lands, who shall testify, who shall have capacity to make a contract in a State, that Congress can also declare by law who, without regard to race or color, shall have the right to act as a juror or as a judge, to hold any office, and finally to vote, in every State and Territory of the United States. As respects the Territories, they come within the power of Congress, for as to them the law-making power is the Federal power; but as to the States, no similar provision exists, vesting in Congress the power to make rules and regulations for them.

"The object of the second section of the bill is to afford discriminating protection to colored persons in the full enjoyment of all the rights secured to them by the preceding section. It declares that 'any person who, under color of any law, statute, ordinance, regulation, or custom, shall subject or cause to be subjected any inhabitant of any State or Territory to the deprivation of any right secured or protected by this act, or to different punishment, pains, or penalties on account of such person having at any time been held in a condition of slavery or involuntary servitude, except as a punishment of crime, whereof the party shall have been duly convicted, or by reason of his color or race, than is prescribed for the punishment of white persons, shall be deemed guilty of a misdemeanor, and on conviction shall be punished by fine not exceeding one thousand dollars, or imprisonment not exceeding one year, or both, in the discretion of the court.' This section seems to be designed to apply to some existing or future law of a State or Territory, which may conflict with the provisions of the bill now under consideration. It provides for counteracting such forbidden legislation, by imposing fine and imprisonment upon the legislators who may pass such conflicting laws, or upon the officers or agents who shall put or attempt to put them into execution. It means an official offence, not a common crime, committed against law upon the person or property of the black race. Such an act may deprive the black man of his property, but not of his right to hold property. It means a deprivation of the right itself, either by the State Judiciary or the State Legislature. It is, therefore, assumed that, under this section, members of a State Legislature who should vote for laws conflicting with the provisions of the bill, that judges of the State courts who should render judgments in antagonism with its terms, and that marshals and sheriffs who should as ministerial officers execute processes sanctioned by State laws and issued by State judges in execution of their judgments, could be brought before other tribunals and there subjected to fine and imprisonment, for the performance of the duties which such State laws might impose. The legislation thus proposed invades the judicial power of the State. It says to every State court or judge: If you decide that this act is unconstitutional; if you hold that over such a subject-matter the said law is paramount, under color of a State law refuse the exercise of the right to the negro; your error of judgment, however conscientious, shall subject you to fine and imprisonment. I do not apprehend that the conflicting legislation which the bill seems to contemplate is so likely to occur, as to render it necessary at this time to adopt a measure of such constitutionality. In the next place, this provision of the bill seems to be unnecessary, as adequate judicial remedies could be adopted to secure the desired end without invading the immunities of legislators, always important to be preserved in the interest of public liberty, notwithstanding the independence of the judiciary, always essential to the preservation of individual rights, and without impairing the efficiency of ministerial officers, always necessary for the maintenance of public peace and order. The remedy proposed by this section seems to be in this respect not only anomalous but unconstitutional, for the Constitution guarantees nothing with certainty if it does not insure to the several States the right of making index ruling laws in regard to all matters arising within their jurisdiction, subject only to the restriction, in cases of conflict with the Constitution and constitutional laws of the United States—the latter to be held as the supreme law of the land.

"The third section gives the district courts of the United States exclusive cognizance of all crimes and offences committed against the provisions of this act, and concurrent jurisdiction with the circuit courts of the United States, of all civil and criminal cases affecting persons that are denied, or cannot enforce in the courts or judicial tribunals of the State or locality where they may be, any of the rights secured to them by the first section. The construction which I have given to the second section is strengthened by this third section, for it makes clear what kind of denial, or deprivation of rights secured by the first section, was in contemplation. It is a denial or deprivation of such rights in the courts or judicial tribunals of the State. It stands, therefore, clear of doubt that the offence and the penalties provided in the second section are intended for the State judge who, in the clear exercise of his functions as a judge, not acting ministerially but judicially, shall decide contrary to this Federal law. In other words, when a State judge, acting upon a question involving a conflict between a State law and a Federal law, and bound, according to his own judgment and responsibility to give an impartial decision between the two, comes to the conclusion that the State law is valid and the Federal law is invalid, he must not follow the dictates of his own judgment, at the peril of fine and imprisonment. The legislative department of the Government of the United States thus takes from the judicial department of the States the sacred and exclusive duty of judicial decision, and converts the State judge into a mere ministerial officer, bound to decide according to the will of Congress. It is clear that in States which deny to persons, whose rights are secured by the first section of the bill, any one of those rights, all criminal and civil cases affecting them will, by the provisions of the third section, come under the executive cognizance of the Federal tribunals. It follows that if in any State, which denies to a colored person any one of all these rights, that person should commit a crime against the laws of a State—murder, arson, rape, or any other crime—all protection and punishment, through the courts of the State, are taken away, and he can only be tried and punished in the Federal courts. How is the criminal to be tried, if the offence is provided for and punished by Federal law? That law, and not the State law, is to govern. It was only when the offence does not happen to be within the province of Federal law that the Federal courts are to try and punish him under any other law. The resort is to be had to the common law, as modified and changed by State legislation, so far as the same is not inconsistent with the Constitution and laws of the United States. So that over this vast domain of criminal jurisprudence, provided by each State for the protection of its citizens and for the punishment of all persons who violate its criminal laws, Federal law, wherever it can be made to apply, displaces State law. The question naturally arises, from what source Congress derives the power to transfer to Federal tribunals certain classes of cases embraced in this section. The Constitution expressly declares that the judicial power of the United States 'shall extend to all cases in law and equity, arising under this Constitution, the laws of the United States, and treaties made, or which shall be made, under their authority; to all cases affecting ambassadors or other public ministers and consuls; to all cases of admiralty and maritime jurisdiction; to controversies to which the United States shall be a party; to controversies between two or more States; between a State and citizens of another State; between citizens of different States; between citizens of the same State claiming land under grants of different States; and between a State, or the citizens thereof, and foreign States, citizens, or subjects.'

"Here the judicial power of the United States is expressly set forth and defined; and the act of September 24, 1789, establishing the judicial courts of the United States, in conferring upon the Federal courts jurisdiction over cases originating in State tribunals, is careful to confine them to the classes enumerated in the above recited clause of the Constitution. This section of the bill undoubtedly comprehends cases and authorizes the exercise of powers that are not, by the Constitution, within the jurisdiction of the courts of the United States. To transfer them to these courts would be an exercise of authority well calculated to excite distrust and alarm on the part of all the States, for the bill applies alike to all of them, as well as to those who have not been engaged in rebellion. It may be assumed that this authority is incident to the power granted to Congress by the Constitution as recently amended, to enforce, by appropriate legislation, the article declaring that neither slavery nor involuntary servitude, except as a punishment for crime, whereof the party shall have been duly convicted, shall exist within the United States, or any place subject to their jurisdiction. It cannot, however, be justly claimed that, with a view to the enforcement of this article of the Constitution, there is at present any necessity for the exercise of all the powers which this bill confers. Slavery has been abolished, and at present nowhere exists within the jurisdiction of the United States. Nor has there been, nor is it likely there will be any attempts to revive it by the people of the States. If, however, any such attempt shall be made, it will then become the duty of the General Government to exercise any and all incidental powers necessary and proper to maintain inviolate this great law of freedom. The fourth section of the bill provides that officers and agents of the Freedmen's Bureau shall be empowered to make arrests, and also that other officers shall be specially commissioned for that purpose by the President of the United States. It also authorizes the Circuit Courts of the United States and the Superior Courts of the Territories to appoint, without limitation, commissioners, who are to be charged with the performance of quasi judicial duties. The fifth section empowers the commissioners so to be selected by the court, to appoint, in writing, one or more suitable persons from time to time to execute warrants and processes desirable by the bill. These numerous official agents are made to constitute a sort of police in addition to the military, and are authorized to summon a *posse commitatus*, and even to call to their aid such portion of the land and naval forces of the United States, or of the militia, 'as may be necessary to the performance of the duty with which they are charged.' This extraordinary power is to be conferred upon agents irresponsible to the Government and to the people, to whose number the discretion of the commissioners is the only limit, and in whose hands such authority might be made a terrible engine of wrong, oppression, and fraud. The general statutes regulating the land and naval forces of the United States, the militia, and the execution of the laws are believed to be adequate for any emergency which can occur in time of peace. If it should prove otherwise, Congress can at any time amend those laws in such a manner as, while subserving the public welfare, not to jeopard the rights, interests, and liberties of the people.

"The seventh section provides that a fee of ten dollars shall be paid to each commissioner in every case brought before him, and a fee of five dollars to his deputy or deputies for each person he or they may arrest and take before any such commissioner in general for performing such other duties as may be required in the premises. All these fees are to be paid out of the Treasury of the United States, whether there is a conviction or not; but in case of conviction they are to be recoverable from the defendant. It seems to me that under the influence of such temptations, bad men might convert any law, however beneficent, into an instrument of persecution and fraud. By the eighth section of the bill, the United States Courts, which sit only in one place for white citizens, must migrate with the marshal and district attorney, and necessarily with the clerk (although he is not mentioned), to any part of the district, upon the order of the President, and there hold a court for the purpose of the more speedy arrest and trial of persons charged with the violation of this act; and there the judge and officers of the court must remain, upon the order of the President, for the time therein designated.

"The ninth section authorizes the President, or such person as he may empower for that purpose, to employ such part of the land or naval forces of the United States, or of the militia, as shall be necessary to prevent the violation and enforce the due execution of this act. This language seems to imply a permanent military force that is to be always at hand, and whose only business is to be the enforcement of this measure over the vast region where it intended to operate.

"I do not propose to consider the policy of this bill. To me the details of the bill are fraught with evil. The white race and black race of the South have hitherto lived together under the relation of master and slave—capital owning labor. Now that relation is changed; and as to ownership, capital and labor are divorced. They stand now, each master of itself. In this new relation, one being necessary to the other, there will be a new adjustment, which both are deeply interested in making harmonious. Each has equal power in settling the terms; and, if left to the laws that regulate capital and labor, it is confidently believed that they will satisfactorily work out the problem. Capital, it is true, has more intelligence; but labor is never so ignorant as not to understand its own interests, not to know its own value, and not to see that capital must pay that value. This bill frustrates this adjustment. It intervenes between capital and labor, and attempts to settle questions of political economy through the agency of numerous officials, whose interest it will be to foment discord between the two races; for as the breach widens, their employment will continue; and when it is closed, their occupation will terminate. In all our history, in all our experience as a people living under Federal and State law, no such system as that contemplated by the details of this bill has ever before been proposed or adopted. They establish for the security of the colored race safeguards which go indefinitely beyond any that the General Government has ever provided for the white race. In fact, the distinction of race and color is by the bill made to operate in favor of the colored and against the white race. They interfere with the municipal legislation of the States; with relations existing exclusively between a State and its citizens, or between inhabitants of the same State; an absorption and assumption of power by the General Government which, if acquiesced in, must sap and destroy our federative system of limited power, and break down the barriers which preserve the rights of the States. It is another step, or rather stride, towards centralization and the concentration of all legislative powers in the National Government. The tendency of the bill must be to resuscitate the spirit of rebellion, and to arrest the progress of those influences which are more closely drawing around the States the bonds of union and peace.

"My lamented predecessor, in his proclamation of the 1st of January, 1863, ordered and declared that all persons held as slaves within certain States and parts of States therein designated, were, and thenceforward should be free; and further, that the Executive Government of the United States, including the military and naval authorities thereof, would recognize and maintain the freedom of such persons. This guaranty has been rendered especially obligatory and sacred by the amendment of the Constitution abolishing slavery throughout the United States. I, therefore, fully recognize the obligation to protect and defend that class of our people whenever and wherever it shall become necessary, and to the full extent, compatible with the Constitution of the United States. Entertaining these sentiments, it only remains for me to say that I will cheerfully co-operate with Congress in any measure that may be necessary for the preservation of civil rights of the freedmen, as well as those of all other classes of persons throughout the United States, by judicial process under equal and impartial laws, or conformably with the provisions of the Federal Constitution.

"I now return the bill to the Senate, and regret that in considering the bills and joint resolutions, forty-two in number, which have been thus far submitted for my approval, I am compelled to withhold my assent from a second measure that has received the sanction of both Houses of Congress.

"ANDREW JOHNSON.

"WASHINGTON, D. C., March 27, 1866."

CHAPTER XVIII.

ANNUAL MESSAGE TO THE THIRTY-NINTH CONGRESS.

"*Fellow-citizens of the Senate and House of Representatives:*

"To express gratitude to God, in the name of the people, for the preservation of the United States, is my first duty in addressing you. Our thoughts next revert to the death of the late President by an act of parricidal treason. The grief of the nation is still fresh; it finds some solace in the consideration that he lived to enjoy the highest proof of its confidence by entering on the renewed term of the Chief Magistracy, to which he had been elected; that he brought the civil war substantially to a close; that his loss was deplored in all parts of the Union; and that foreign nations have rendered justice to his memory. His removal cast upon me a heavier weight of cares than ever devolved upon any one of his predecessors. To fulfil my trust I need the support and confidence of all who are associated with me in the various departments of the Government, and support and confidence of the people. There is but one way in which I can hope to gain their necessary aid; it is, to state with frankness the principles which guide my conduct, and their application to the present state of affairs, well aware that the efficiency of my labors will, in a great measure, depend on your and their undivided approbation.

"The Union of the United States of America was intended by its authors to last as long as the States themselves shall last. 'THE UNION SHALL BE PERPETUAL,' are the words of the Confederation. 'TO FORM A MORE PERFECT UNION,' by an ordinance of the people of the United States, is the declared purpose of the Constitution. The hand of Divine Providence was never more plainly visible in the affairs of men than in the framing and the adopting of that instrument. It is, beyond comparison, the greatest event in American history; and indeed is it not, of all events in modern times, the most pregnant with consequences for every people of the earth? The members of the Convention which prepared it, brought to their work the experience of the Confederation, of their several States, and of other republican governments, old and new; but they needed and they obtained a wisdom superior to experience. And when for its validity it required the approval of a people that occupied a large part of a continent and acted separately in many distinct conventions, what is more wonderful than that, after earnest contention and long discussion, all feelings and all opinions were ultimately drawn in one way to its support?

"The Constitution to which life was thus imparted contains within itself ample resources for its own preservation. It has power to enforce the laws, punish treason, and insure domestic tranquillity. In case of the usurpation of the Government of a State by one man, or an oligarchy, it becomes a duty of the United

States to make good the guaranty to that State of a republican form of government, and so to maintain the homogeneousness of all. Does the lapse of time reveal defects? A simple mode of amendment is provided in the Constitution itself, so that its conditions can always be made to conform to the requirements of advancing civilization. No room is allowed even for the thought of a possibility of its coming to an end. And these powers of self-preservation have always been asserted in their complete integrity by every patriotic Chief Magistrate—by Jefferson and Jackson, not less than by Washington and Madison. The parting advice of the Father of his Country, while yet President, to the people of the United States, was, that 'the free Constitution, which was the work of their hands, might be sacredly maintained;' and the inaugural words of President Jefferson held up 'the preservation of the General Government, in its constitutional vigor, as the sheet anchor of our peace at home and safety abroad.' The Constitution is the work of 'the People of the United States,' and it should be as indestructible as the people.

"It is not strange that the framers of the Constitution, which had no model in the past, should not have fully comprehended the excellence of their own work. Fresh from a struggle against arbitrary power, many patriots suffered from harassing fears of an absorption of the State Governments by the General Government, and many from a dread that the States would break away from their orbits. But the very greatness of our country should allay the apprehension of encroachments by the General Government. The subjects that come unquestionably within its jurisdiction are so numerous, that it must ever naturally refuse to be embarrassed by questions that lie beyond it. Were it otherwise, the Executive would sink beneath the burden; the channels of justice would be choked; legislation would be obstructed by excess; so that there is a greater temptation to exercise some of the functions of the General Government through the States than to trespass on their rightful sphere. 'The absolute acquiescence in the decisions of the majority' was, at the beginning of the century, enforced by Jefferson 'as the vital principle of republics,' and the events of the last four years have established, we will hope forever, that there lies no appeal to force.

"The maintenance of the Union brings with it 'the support of the State Governments in all their rights;' but it is not one of the rights of any State Government to renounce its own place in the Union, or to nullify the laws of the Union. The largest liberty is to be maintained in the discussion of the acts of the Federal Government; but there is no appeal from its laws, except to the various branches of that Government itself, or to the people, who grant to the members of the Legislative and of the Executive Departments no tenure but a limited one, and in that manner always retain the powers of redress.

"'The sovereignty of the States' is the language of the Confederacy, and not the language of the Constitution. The latter contains the emphatic words: 'The Constitution, and the laws of the United States which shall be made in pursuance thereof, and all treaties made or which shall be made under the authority of the United States, shall be the supreme law of the land; and the judges in every State shall be bound thereby, any thing in the constitution or laws of any State to the contrary notwithstanding.'

"Certainly the Government of the United States is a limited government; and so is every State government a limited government. With us, this idea of limitation spreads through every form of administration, general, State, and municipal, and rests on the great distinguishing principle of the recognition of the rights of man. The ancient republics absorbed the individual in the State, prescribed his religion, and controlled his activity. The American system rests on the assertion of the equal right of every man to life, liberty, and the pursuit of happiness; to freedom of conscience, to the culture and exercise of all his faculties. As a consequence, the State Government is limited, as to the General Government in the interest of the Union, as to the individual citizen in the interest of freedom.

"States, with proper limitations of power, are essential to the existence of the Constitution of the United States. At the very commencement, when we assumed a place among the powers of the earth, the Declaration of Independence was adopted by States; so also were the Articles of Confederation; and when 'the People of the United States' ordained and established the Constitution, it was the assent of the States, one by one, which gave it vitality. In the event, too, of any amendment to the Constitution, the proposition of Congress needs the confirmation of States. Without States, one great branch of the legislative government would be wanting. And, if we look beyond the letter of the Constitution to the character of our country, its capacity for comprehending within its jurisdiction a vast continental empire is due to the system of States. The best security for the perpetual existence of the States is the 'supreme authority' of the Constitution of the United States. The perpetuity of the Constitution brings with it the perpetuity of the States ; their mutual relation makes us what we are, and in our political system their connection is indissoluble. The whole cannot exist without the parts, nor the parts without the whole. So long as the Constitution of the United States endures, the States will endure : the destruction of the one is the destruction of the other ; the preservation of the one is the preservation of the other.

"I have thus explained my views of the mutual relations of the Constitution and the States, because they unfold the principles on which I have sought to solve the momentous questions and overcome the appalling difficulties that met me at the very commencement of my administration. It has been my steadfast object to escape from the sway of momentary passions, and to derive a healing policy from the fundamental and unchanging principles of the Constitution.

"I found the States suffering from the effects of a civil war. Resistance to the General Government appeared to have exhausted itself. The United States had recovered possession of their forts and arsenals ; and their armies were in the occupation of every State which had attempted to secede. Whether the territory within the limits of those States should be held as conquered territory, under military authority emanating from the President as the head of the army, was the first question that presented itself for decision.

"Now, military governments, established for an indefinite period, would have offered no security for the early suppression of discontent; would have divided the people into the vanquishers and the vanquished; and would have envenomed hatred, rather than have restored affection. Once established, no precise limit to their continuance was conceivable. They would have occasioned an incalculable and exhausting expense. Peaceful emigration to and from that portion of the country is one of the best means that can be thought of for the restoration of harmony; and that emigration would have been prevented; for what emigrant from abroad, what industrious citizen at home, would place himself willingly under military rule? The chief persons who would have followed in the train of the army would have been dependents on the General Government, or men who expected profit from the miseries of their erring fellow-citizens. The powers of patronage and rule which would have been exercised, under the President, over a vast, and populous, and naturally wealthy region, are greater than, unless under extreme necessity, I should be willing to intrust to any one man; they are such as, for myself, I could never, unless on occasions of great emergency, consent to exercise. The wilful use of such powers, if continued through a period of years, would have endangered the purity of the general administration and the liberties of the States which remained loyal.

"Besides, the policy of military rule over a conquered territory would have implied that the States whose inhabitants may have taken part in the rebellion had, by the act of those inhabitants, ceased to exist. But the true theory is, that all pretended acts of secession were, from the beginning, null and void. The States cannot commit treason, nor screen the individual citizens who may have committed treason, any more than they can make valid treaties or engage in lawful commerce with any foreign power. The States attempting to secede placed themselves in a condition where their vitality was impaired, but not extinguished—their functions suspended, but not destroyed.

"But if any State neglects or refuses to perform its offices, there is the more need that the General Government should maintain all its authority, and, as soon as practicable, resume the exercise of all its functions. On this principle I have acted, and have gradually and quietly, and by almost imperceptible steps, sought to restore the rightful energy of the General Government and of the States. To that end, Provisional Governors have been appointed for the States, conventions called, Governors elected, Legislatures assembled, and Senators and Representatives chosen to the Congress of the United States. At the same time, the courts of the United States, as far as could be done, have been reopened, so that the laws of the United States may be enforced through their agency. The blockade has been removed and the custom-houses re-established in ports of entry, so that the revenue of the United States may be collected. The Post-office Department renews its ceaseless activity, and the General Government is thereby enabled to communicate promptly with its officers and agents. The courts bring security to persons and property; the opening of the ports invites the restoration of industry and commerce; the post-office renews the facilities of social intercourse and of business. And is it not happy for us all, that the restoration of each one of these functions of the General Government brings with it a blessing to the States over which they are extended? Is it not a sure promise of harmony and renewed attachment to the Union, that, after all that has happened, the return of the General Government is known only as a beneficence?

"I know very well that this policy is attended with some risk; that for its success it requires at least the acquiescence of the States which it concerns; that it implies an invitation to those States, by renewing their allegiance to the United States, to resume their functions as States of the Union. But it is a risk that must be taken; in the choice of difficulties, it is the smallest risk; and to diminish, and, if possible, to remove all danger, I have felt it encumbent on me to assert one other power of the General Government—the power of pardon. As no State can throw a defence over the crime of treason, the power of pardon is exclusively vested in the Executive Government of the United States. In exercising that power, I have taken every precaution to connect it with the clearest recognition of the binding force of the laws of the United States, and an unqualified acknowledgment of the great social change of condition in regard to slavery which has grown out of the war.

"The next step which I have taken to restore the constitutional relations of the States, has been an invitation to them to participate in the high office of amending the Constitution. Every patriot must wish for a general amnesty at the earliest epoch consistent with public safety. For this great end there is need of a concurrence of all opinions, and the spirit of mutual conciliation. All parties in the late terrible conflict must work together in harmony. It is not too much to ask, in the name of the whole people, that, on the one side, the plan of restoration shall proceed in conformity with a willingness to cast the disorders of the past into oblivion; and that, on the other, the evidence of sincerity in the future maintenance of the Union shall be put beyond any doubt by the ratification of the proposed amendment to the Constitution, which provides for the abolition of slavery forever within the limits of our country. So long as the adoption of this amendment is delayed, so long will doubt, and jealousy, and uncertainty prevail. This is the measure which will efface the sad memory of the past; this is the measure which will most certainly call population, and capital, and security to those parts of the Union that need them most. Indeed, it is not too much to ask of the States which are now resuming their places in the family of the Union, to give this pledge of perpetual loyalty and peace. Until it is done, the past, however much we may desire it, will not be forgotten. The adoption of the amendment reunites us beyond all power of disruption. It heals the wound that is still imperfectly closed; it removes slavery, the element which has so long perplexed and divided the country; it makes of us once more a united people, renewed and strengthened, bound more than ever to mutual affection and support.

"The amendment to the Constitution being adopted, it would remain for the States, whose powers have been so long in abeyance, to resume their places in the two branches of the National Legislature, and thereby complete the work of restoration. Here it is for you, fellow-citizens of the Senate, and for you, fellow-citizens of the House of Representatives, to judge, each of you for yourselves, of the elections, returns, and qualifications of your own members.

"The full assertion of the powers of the General Government requires the holding of circuit courts of the United States within the districts where their authority has been interrupted. In the present posture of our public affairs, strong objections have been urged to holding those courts in any of the States where the rebellion has existed; and it was ascertained, by inquiry, that the Circuit Court of the United States would not be held within the District of Virginia during the autumn or early winter, nor until Congress should have 'an opportunity to consider and act on the whole subject.' To your deliberations the restoration of this branch of the civil authority of the United States is therefore necessarily referred, with the hope that early provision will be made for the resumption of all its functions. It is manifest that treason, most flagrant in character, has been committed. Persons who are charged with its commission should have fair and impartial trials in the highest civil tribunals of the country, in order that the Constitution and the laws may be fully vindicated; the truth clearly established and affirmed that treason is a crime, that traitors should be punished and the offence made infamous; and, at the same time, that the question may be judicially settled, finally and forever, that no State, of its own will, has the right to renounce its place in the Union.

"The relations of the General Government towards the four millions of inhabitants, whom the war has called into freedom, have engaged my most serious consideration. On the propriety of attempting to make the freedmen electors by the proclamation of the Executive, I took for my counsel the Constitution itself, the interpretations of that instrument by its authors and their contemporaries, and recent legislation by Congress. When, at the first movement towards independence, the Congress of the United States instructed the several States to institute governments of their own, they left each State to decide for itself the conditions for the enjoyment of the elective franchise. During the period of the confederacy, there continued to exist a very great diversity in the qualifications of electors in the several States; and even within a State a distinction of qualifications prevailed with regard to the officers who were to be chosen. The Constitution of the United States recognizes these diversities when it enjoins that, in the choice of members of the House of Representatives of the United States, 'the electors in each State shall have the qualifications requisite for electors of the most numerous branch of the State Legislature.' After the formation of the Constitution, it remained, as before, the uniform usage for each State to enlarge the body of its electors, according to its own judgment; and, under this system, one State after another has proceeded to increase the number of its electors, until now universal suffrage, or something very near it, is the general rule. So fixed was this reservation of power in the habits of the people, and so unquestioned has been the interpretation of the Constitution, that during the civil war the late President never harbored the purpose—certainly never avowed the purpose—of disregarding it; and in the acts of Congress, during that period, nothing can be found which, during the continuance of hostilities, much less after their close, would have sanctioned any departure by the Executive from a policy which has so uniformly obtained. Moreover, a concession of the elective franchise to the freedmen, by act of the President of the United States, must have been extended to all colored men, wherever found, and so must have established a change of suffrage in the Northern, Middle, and Western States, not less than in the Southern and Southwestern. Such an act would have created a new class of voters, and would have been an assumption of power by the President which nothing in the Constitution or laws of the United States would have warranted.

"On the other hand, every danger of conflict is avoided when the settlement of the question is referred to the several States. They can, each for itself, decide on the measure, and whether it is to be adopted at once and absolutely, or introduced gradually and with conditions. In my judgment, the freedmen, if they show patience and manly virtues, will sooner obtain a participation in the elective franchise through the States than through the General Government, even if it had power to intervene. When the tumult of emotions that have been raised by the suddenness of the social change shall have subsided, it may prove that they will receive the kindliest usage from some of those on whom they have heretofore most closely depended.

"But while I have no doubt that now, after the close of the war, it is not competent for the General Government to extend the elective franchise in the several States, it is equally clear that good faith requires the security of the freedmen in their liberty and their property, their right to labor, and their right to claim the just return of their labor. I cannot too strongly urge a dispassionate treatment of this subject, which should be carefully kept aloof from all party strife. We must equally avoid hasty assumptions of any natural impossibility for the two races to live side by side, in a state of mutual benefit and good-will. The experiment involves us in no inconsistency; let us, then, go on and make that experiment in good faith, and not be too easily disheartened. The country is in need of labor, and the freedmen are in need of employment, culture, and protection. While their right of voluntary migration and expatriation is not to be questioned, I would not advise their forced removal and colonization. Let us rather encourage them to honorable and useful industry, where it may be beneficial to themselves and to the country; and, instead of hasty anticipations of the certainty of failure, let there be nothing wanting to the fair trial of the experiment. The change in their condition is the substitution of labor by contract for the status of slavery. The freedman cannot fairly be accused of unwillingness to work, so long as a doubt remains about his freedom of choice in his pursuits, and the certainty of his recovering his stipulated wages. In this the interests of the employer and the employed coincide.

The employer desires in his workmen spirit and alacrity, and these can be permanently secured in no other way. And if the one ought to be able to enforce the contract, so ought the other. The public interest will be best promoted, if the several States will provide adequate protection and remedies for the freedmen. Until this is in some way accomplished, there is no chance for the advantageous use of their labor; and the blame of ill-success will not rest on them.

"I know that sincere philanthropy is earnest for the immediate realization of its remotest aims; but time is always an element in reform. It is one of the greatest acts on record to have brought four millions of people into freedom. The career of free industry must be fairly opened to them; and then their future prosperity and condition must, after all, rest mainly on themselves. If they fail, and so perish away, let us be careful that the failure shall not be attributable to any denial of justice. In all that relates to the destiny of the freedmen, we need not be too anxious to read the future; many incidents which, from a speculative point of view, might raise alarm, will quietly settle themselves.

"Now that slavery is at an end, or near its end, the greatness of its evil, in the point of view of public economy, becomes more and more apparent. Slavery was essentially a monopoly of labor, and as such locked the States where it prevailed against the incoming of free industry. Where labor was the property of the capitalist, the white man was excluded from employment, or had but the second best chance of finding it; and the foreign emigrant turned away from the region where his condition would be so precarious. With the destruction of the monopoly, free labor will hasten from all parts of the civilized world to assist in developing various and immeasurable resources which have hitherto lain dormant. The eight or nine States nearest the Gulf of Mexico have a soil of exuberant fertility, a climate friendly to long life, and can sustain a denser population than is found as yet in any part of our country. And the future influx of population to them will be mainly from the North, or from the most cultivated nations in Europe. From the sufferings that have attended them during our late struggle, let us look away to the future, which is sure to be laden for them with greater prosperity than has ever before been known. The removal of the monopoly of slave labor is a pledge that those regions will be peopled by a numerous and enterprising population, which will vie with any in the Union in compactness, inventive genius, wealth, and industry.

"Our Government springs from and was made for the people—not the people for the Government. To them it owes allegiance; from them it must derive its courage, strength, and wisdom. But, while the Government is thus bound to defer to the people, from whom it derives its existence, it should, from the very consideration of its origin, be strong in its power of resistance to the establishment of inequalities. Monopolies, perpetuities, and class legislation are contrary to the genius of free government, and ought not to be allowed. Here, there is no room for favored classes or monopolies: the principle of our Government is that of equal laws and freedom of industry. Wherever a monopoly attains a foothold, it is sure to be a source of danger, discord, and trouble. We shall but fulfil our duties as legislators by according 'equal and exact justice to all men,' special privileges to none. The Government is subordinate to the people; but, as the agent and representative of the people, it must be held superior to monopolies, which, in themselves, ought never to be granted, and which, where they exist, must be subordinate and yield to the Government.

"The Constitution confers on Congress the right to regulate commerce among the several States. It is of the first necessity, for the maintenance of the Union, that that commerce should be free and unobstructed. No State can be justified in any device to tax the transit of travel and commerce between States. The position of many States is such that, if they were allowed to take advantage of it for purposes of local revenue, the commerce between States might be injuriously burdened, or even virtually prohibited. It is best, while the country is still young, and while the tendency to dangerous monopolies of this kind is still feeble, to use the power of Congress so as to prevent any selfish impediment to the free circulation of men and merchandise. A tax on travel and merchandise, in their transit, constitutes one of the worst forms of monopoly, and the evil is increased if coupled with a denial of the choice of route. When the vast extent of our country is considered, it is plain that every obstacle to the free circulation of commerce between the States ought to be sternly guarded against by appropriate legislation, within the limits of the Constitution.

"The report of the Secretary of the Interior explains the condition of the public lands, the transactions of the Patent Office and the Pension Bureau, the management of our Indian affairs, the progress made in the construction of the Pacific railroad, and furnishes information in reference to matters of local interest in the District of Columbia. It also presents evidence of the successful operation of the Homestead Act, under the provisions of which 1,160,533 acres of the public lands were entered during the last fiscal year—more than one-fourth of the whole number of acres sold or otherwise disposed of during that period. It is estimated that the receipts derived from this source are sufficient to cover the expenses incident to the survey and disposal of the lands entered under this act, and that payments in cash to the extent of from forty to fifty per cent. will be made by settlers, who may thus at any time acquire title before the expiration of the period at which it would otherwise vest. The homestead policy was established only after long and earnest resistance: experience proves its wisdom. The lands, in the hands of industrious settlers, whose labor creates wealth and contributes to the public resources, are worth more to the United States than if they had been reserved as a solitude for future purchasers.

"The lamentable events of the last four years, and the sacrifices made by the gallant men of our army and navy, have swelled the records of the Pension Bureau to an unprecedented extent. On the 30th day of June last, the total number of pensioners was 85,986, requiring for their annual pay, exclusive of expenses, the sum of $8,023,445. The number of applications that have been allowed since that date will require a large increase of this amount for the next fiscal year. The means for the payment of the stipends due, under existing laws, to our disabled soldiers and sailors, and to the families of such as have perished in the service of the country, will no doubt be cheerfully and promptly granted. A grateful people will not hesitate to sanction any measures having for their object the relief of soldiers mutilated and families made fatherless in the efforts to preserve our national existence.

"The report of the postmaster-general presents an encouraging exhibit of the operations of the Post-office Department during the year. The revenues of the past year from the loyal States alone exceeded the maximum annual receipts from all the States previous to the rebellion, in the sum of $6,038,091; and the annual average increase of revenue during the last four years, compared with the revenues of the four years immediately preceding the rebellion, was $3,533,845. The revenues of the last fiscal year amounted to $14,556,158, and the expenditures to $13,694,728, leaving a surplus of receipts over expenditures of $861,430. Progress has been made in restoring the postal service in the Southern States. The views presented by the postmaster-general against the policy of granting subsidies to ocean mail steamship lines upon established routes, and in favor of continuing the present system, which limits the compensation for ocean service to the postage earnings, are recommended to the careful consideration of Congress.

"It appears, from the report of the Secretary of the Navy, that while, at the commencement of the present year, there were in commission 530 vessels of all descriptions, armed with 3,000 guns and manned by 51,000 men, the number of vessels at present in commission is 117, with 830 guns and 12,128 men. By this prompt reduction of the naval forces the expenses of the Government have been largely diminished, and a number of vessels, purchased for naval purposes from the merchant marine, have been returned to the peaceful pursuits of commerce. Since the suppression of active hostilities our foreign squadrons have been re-established, and consist of vessels much more efficient than those employed on similar service previous to the rebellion. The suggestion for the enlargement of the navy-yards, and especially for the establishment of one in fresh water for iron-clad vessels, is deserving of consideration, as is also the recommendation for a different location and more ample grounds for the naval academy.

"In the report of the Secretary of War, a general summary is given of the military campaigns of 1864 and 1865, ending in the suppression of armed resistance to the national authority in the insurgent States. The operations of the general administrative bureaus of the War Department during the past year are detailed, and an estimate made of the appropriations that will be required for military purposes in the fiscal year commencing the 30th day of June, 1866. The national military force on the 1st of May, 1865, numbered 1,000,516 men. It is proposed to reduce the military establishment to a peace footing, comprehending fifty thousand troops of all arms, organized so as to admit of an enlargement by filling up the ranks to eighty-two thousand six hundred, if the circumstances of the country should require an augmentation of the army. The volunteer force has already been reduced by the discharge from service of over eight hundred thousand troops, and the department is proceeding rapidly in the work of further reduction. The war estimates are reduced from $516,240,131 to $33,814,461, which amount, in the opinion of the department, is adequate for a peace establishment. The measures of retrenchment in each bureau and branch of the service exhibit a diligent economy worthy of commendation. Reference is also made in the report to the necessity of providing for a uniform militia system, and to the propriety of making suitable provision for wounded and disabled officers and soldiers.

"The revenue system of the country is a subject of vital interest to its honor and prosperity, and should command the earnest consideration of Congress. The Secretary of the Treasury will lay before you a full and detailed report of the receipts and disbursements of the last fiscal year, of the first quarter of the present fiscal year, of the probable receipts and expenditures for the other three quarters, and the estimates for the year following the 30th of June, 1866. I might content myself with a reference to that report, in which you will find all the information required for your deliberations and decision. But the paramount importance of the subject so presses itself on my own mind, that I cannot but lay before you my views of the measures which are required for the good character, and, I might almost say, for the existence of this people. The life of a republic lies certainly in the energy, virtue, and intelligence of its citizens; but it is equally true that a good revenue system is the life of an organized government. I meet you at a time when the nation has voluntarily burdened itself with a debt unprecedented in our annals. Vast as is its amount, it fades away into nothing when compared with the countless blessings that will be conferred upon our country and upon man by the preservation of the nation's life. Now, on the first occasion of the meeting of Congress since the return of peace, it is of the utmost importance to inaugurate a just policy, which shall at once be put in motion, and which shall commend itself to those who come after us for its continuance. We must aim at nothing less than the complete effacement of the financial evils that necessarily follow a state of civil war. We must endeavor to apply the earliest remedy to the deranged state of the currency, and not shrink from devising a policy which, without being oppressive to the people, shall immediately begin to effect a reduction of the debt, and, if persisted in, discharge it fully within a definitely fixed number of years.

"It is our first duty to prepare in earnest for our recovery from the ever-increasing evils of an irredeemable currency, without a sudden revulsion, and yet without untimely procrastination. For that end, we must, each in our respective positions, prepare the way. I hold it the duty of the Executive to insist upon frugality in the expenditures; and a sparing economy is itself a great national resource. Of the banks to which authority has been given to issue notes secured by bonds of the United States, we may require the greatest moderation and prudence, and the law must be rigidly enforced when its limits are exceeded. We may, each one of us, counsel our active and enterprising countrymen to be constantly on their guard, to liquidate debts contracted in a paper currency, and, by conducting business as nearly as possible on a system of cash payments or short credits, to hold themselves prepared to return to the standard of gold and silver. To aid our fellow-citizens in the prudent management of their monetary affairs, the duty devolves on us to diminish by law the amount of paper money now in circulation. Five years ago the bank-note circulation of the country amounted to not much more than two hundred millions; now the circulation, bank and national, exceeds seven hundred millions. The simple statement of this fact recommends more strongly than any words of mine could do, the necessity of our restraining this expansion. The gradual reduction of the currency is the only measure that can save the business of the country from disastrous calamities; and this can be almost imperceptibly accomplished by gradually funding the national circulation in securities that may be made redeemable at the pleasure of the Government.

"Our debt is doubly secure—first in the actual wealth and still greater undeveloped resources of the country; and next in the character of our institutions. The most intelligent observers among political economists have not failed to remark, that the public debt of a country is safe in proportion as its people are free; that the debt of a republic is the safest of all. Our history confirms and establishes the theory, and is, I firmly believe, destined to give it a still more signal illustration. The secret of this superiority springs not merely from the fact that in a republic the national obligations are distributed more widely through countless numbers in all classes of society; it has its root in the character of our laws. Here all men contribute to the public welfare, and bear their fair share of the public burdens. During the war, under the impulses of patriotism, the men of the great body of the people, without regard to their own comparative want of wealth, thronged to our armies and filled our fleets of war, and held themselves ready to offer their lives for the public good. Now, in their turn, the property and income of the country should bear their just proportion of the burden of taxation, while in our impost system, through means of which increased vitality is incidentally imparted to all the industrial interests of the nation, the duties should be so adjusted as to fall most heavily on articles of luxury, leaving the necessaries of life as free from taxation as the absolute wants of the Government, economically administered, will justify. No favored class should demand freedom from assessment, and the taxes should be so distributed as not to fall unduly on the poor, but rather on the accumulated wealth of the country. We should look at the national debt just as it is—not as a national blessing, but as a heavy burden on the industry of the country, to be discharged without unnecessary delay.

"It is estimated by the Secretary of the Treasury that the expenditures for the fiscal year ending the 30th of June, 1866, will exceed the receipts $112,194,947. It is gratifying, however, to state that it is also estimated that the revenue for the year ending the 30th of June, 1867, will exceed the expenditures in the sum of $111,682,818. This amount, or so much as may be deemed sufficient for the purpose, may be applied to the reduction of the public debt, which, on the 31st day of October, 1865, was $2,740,854,750. Every reduction will diminish the total amount of interest to be paid, and so enlarge the means of still further reductions, until the whole shall be liquidated; and this, as will be seen from the estimates of the Secretary of the Treasury, may be accomplished by annual payments even within a period not exceeding thirty years. I have faith that we shall do all this within a reasonable time; that, as we have amazed the world by the suppression of a civil war which was thought to be beyond the control of any Government, so we shall equally show the superiority of our institutions by the prompt and faithful discharge of our national obligations.

"The Department of Agriculture, under its present direction, is accomplishing much in developing and utilizing the vast agricultural capabilities of the country, and for information respecting the details of its management reference is made to the annual report of the Commissioner.

"I have dwelt thus fully on our domestic affairs because of their transcendent importance. Under any circumstances, our great extent of territory and variety of climate, producing almost every thing that is necessary for the wants, and even the comforts of man, make us singularly independent of the varying policy of foreign powers, and protect us against every temptation to 'entangling alliances;' while at the present moment the re-establishment of harmony, and the strength that comes from harmony, will be our best security against 'nations who feel power and forget right.' For myself, it has been and it will be my constant aim to promote peace and amity with all foreign nations and powers; and I have every reason to believe that they all, without exception, are animated by the same disposition. Our relations with the Emperor of China, so recent in their origin, are most friendly. Our commerce with his dominions is receiving new developments; and it is very pleasing to find that the Government of that great empire manifests satisfaction with our policy, and reposes just confidence in the fairness which marks our intercourse. The unbroken harmony between the United States and the Emperor of Russia is receiving a new support from an enterprise designed to carry the telegraphic lines across the continent of Asia, through his dominions, and so to connect us with all Europe by a new channel of intercourse. Our commerce with South America is about to receive encouragement by a direct line of mail steamships to the rising Empire of Brazil. The distinguished party of men of science who have recently left our country to make a scientific exploration of the natural history and rivers and mountain ranges of that region, have received from the emperor that generous welcome which was to have been expected from his constant friendship for the United States, and his well-known zeal in promoting the advancement of knowledge. A hope is entertained that our commerce with the rich and populous countries that border the Mediterranean sea may be largely increased. Nothing will be wanting, on the part of this Government, to extend the protection of our flag over the enterprise of our fellow-citizens. We receive from the powers in that region assurances of good-will; and it is worthy of note that a special envoy has brought us messages of condolence on the death of our late Chief Magistrate from the Bey of Tunis, whose rule includes the old dominions of Carthage, on the African coast.

"Our domestic contest, now happily ended, has left some traces in our relations with one at least of the great maritime powers. The formal accordance of belligerent rights to the insurgent States was unprecedented, and has not been justified by the issue. But in the systems of neutrality pursued by the powers which made that concession, there was a marked difference. The materials of war for the insurgent States were furnished, in a great measure, from the workshops of Great Britain; and British ships, manned by British subjects, and prepared for receiving British armaments, sailed from the ports of Great Britain to make war on American commerce, under the shelter of a commission from the insurgent States. These ships, having once escaped from British ports, ever afterwards entered them in every part of the world, to refit, and so to renew their depredations. The consequences of this conduct were most disastrous to the States then in rebellion, increasing their desolation and misery by the prolongation of our civil contest. It had, moreover, the effect, to a great extent, to drive the American flag from the sea, and to transfer much of our shipping and commerce to the very power whose subjects had created the necessity for such a change. These events took place before I was called to the administration of the Government. The sincere desire for peace by which I am animated, led me to approve the proposal, already made, to submit the questions which had thus arisen between the countries to arbitration. These questions are of such moment that they must have commanded the attention of the great powers, and are so interwoven with the peace and interests of every one of them as to have insured an impartial decision. I regret to inform you that Great Britain declined the arbitrament, but, on the other hand, invited us to the formation of a joint commission to settle mutual claims between the two countries, from which those for the depredations before-mentioned should be excluded. The proposition, in that very unsatisfactory form, has been declined.

"The United States did not present the subject as an impeachment of the good faith of a power which was professing the most friendly dispositions, but as involving questions of public law, of which the settlement is essential to the peace of nations; and, though pecuniary reparation to their injured citizens would have followed incidentally on a decision against Great Britain, such compensation was not their primary object. They had a higher motive, and it was in the interests of peace and justice to establish important principles of international law. The correspondence will be placed before you. The ground on which the British Minister rests his justification is, substantially, that the municipal law of a nation, and the domestic interpretations of that law, are the measure of its duty as a neutral; and I feel bound to declare my opinion, before you and before the world, that that justification cannot be sustained before the tribunal of nations. At the same time, I do not advise to any present attempt at redress by acts of legislation. For the future, friendship between the two countries must rest on the basis of mutual justice.

"From the moment of the establishment of our free Constitution, the civilized world has been convulsed by revolutions in the interests of democracy or of monarchy ; but through all those revolutions the United States have wisely and firmly refused to become propagandists of republicanism. It is the only government suited to our condition; but we have never sought to impose it on others; and we have consistently followed the advice of Washington, to recommend it only by the careful preservation and prudent use of the blessing. During all the intervening period the policy of European powers and of the United States has, on the whole, been harmonious. Twice, indeed, rumors of the invasion of some parts of America, in the interest of monarchy, have prevailed; twice my predecessors have had occasion to announce the views of this nation in respect to such interference. On both occasions the remonstrance of the United States was respected, from a deep conviction, on the part of European governments, that the system of non-interference and mutual abstinence from propagandism was the true rule for the two hemispheres. Since those times we have advanced in wealth and power; but we retain the same purpose to leave the nations of Europe to choose their own dynasties and form their own systems of government. This consistent moderation may justly demand a corresponding moderation. We should regard it as a great calamity to ourselves, to the cause of good government, and to the peace of the world, should any European power challenge the American people, as it were, to the defence of republicanism against foreign interference. We cannot foresee; and are unwilling to consider, what opportunities might present themselves, what combinations might offer to protect ourselves against designs inimical to our form of government. The United States desire to act in the future as they have ever acted heretofore; they never will be driven from that course but by the aggression of European powers; and we rely on the wisdom and justice of those powers to respect the system of non-interference which has so long been sanctioned by time, and which, by its good results, has approved itself to both continents.

"The correspondence between the United States and France, in reference to questions which have become subjects of discussion between the two Governments, will, at a proper time, be laid before Congress.

"When, on the organization of our Government, under the Constitution, the President of the United States delivered his inaugural address to the two Houses of Congress, he said to them, and through them to the country and to mankind: 'The preservation of the sacred fire of liberty and the destiny of the republican model of government, are justly considered as deeply, perhaps as finally staked on the experiment intrusted to the American people.' And the House of Representatives answered Washington by the voice of Madison: 'We adore the invisible hand which has led the American people, through so many difficulties, to cherish a conscious responsibility for the destiny of republican liberty.' More than seventy-six years have glided away since these words were spoken; the United States have passed through severer trials than were foreseen; and now, at this new epoch in our existence as one nation, with our Union purified by sorrows, and strengthened by conflict, and established by the virtue of the people, the greatness of the occasion invites us once more to repeat, with solemnity, the pledges of our fathers to hold ourselves answerable before our fellow-men for the success of the republican form of government. Experience has proved its sufficiency in peace and in war; it has vindicated its authority through dangers, and afflictions, and sudden and terrible emergencies, which would have crushed any system that had been less firmly fixed in the heart of the people. At the inauguration of Washington the foreign relations of the country were few, and its trade was repressed by hostile regulations; now, all the civilized nations of the globe welcome our commerce, and their Governments profess towards us amity. Then our country felt its way hesitatingly along an untried path, with States so little bound together by rapid means of communication as to be hardly known to one another, and with historic traditions extending over very few years; now intercourse between the States is swift and intimate; the experience of centuries has been crowded into a few generations, and has created an intense, indestructible nationality. Then our jurisdiction did not reach beyond the inconvenient boundaries of the territory which had achieved independence; now, through cessions of lands, first colonized by Spain and France, the country has acquired a more complex character, and has for its natural limits the chain of lakes, the Gulf of Mexico, and on the east and the west the two great oceans. Other nations were wasted by civil wars for ages before they could establish for themselves the necessary degree of unity; the latent conviction that our form of government is the best ever known to the world, has enabled us to emerge from civil war within four years, with a complete vindication of the constitutional authority of the General Government, and with our local liberties and State institutions unimpaired. The throngs of emigrants that crowd to our shores are witnesses of the confidence of all peoples in our permanence. Here is the great land of free labor, where industry is blessed with unexampled rewards, and the bread of the workingman is sweetened by the consciousness that the cause of the country 'is his own cause, his own safety, his own dignity.' Here every one enjoys the free use of his faculties and the choice of activity as a natural right. Here, under the combined influence of a fruitful soil, genial climes, and happy institutions, population has increased fifteen-fold within a century. Here, through the easy development of boundless resources, wealth has increased with twofold greater rapidity than numbers, so that we have become secure against the financial vicissitudes of other countries, and, alike in business and in opinion, are self-centred and truly independent. Here more and more care is given to provide education for every one born on our soil. Here religion, released from political connection with the civil government, refuses to subserve the craft of statesmen, and becomes, in its independence, the spiritual life of the people. Here toleration is extended to every opinion, in the quiet certainty that truth needs only a fair field to secure the victory. Here the human mind goes forth unshackled in the pursuit of science, to collect stores of knowledge and acquire an ever-increasing mastery over the forces of nature. Here the national domain is offered and held in millions of separate freeholds, so that our fellow-citizens, beyond the occupants of any other part of the earth, constitute in reality a people. Here exists the democratic form of government; and that form of government, by the confession of European statesmen, 'gives a power of which no other form is capable, because it incorporates every man with the State, and arouses every thing that belongs to the soul.'

"Where, in past history, does a parallel exist to the public happiness which is within the reach of the people of the United States? Where, in any part of the globe, can institutions be found so suited to their habits or so entitled to their love as their own free Constitution? Every one of them, then, in whatever part of the land he has his home, must wish its perpetuity. Who of them will not now acknowledge, in the words of Washington, that 'every step by which the people of the United States have advanced to the character of an independent nation, seems to have been distinguished by some token of Providential agency?' Who will not join with me in the prayer, that the invisible hand which has led us through the clouds that gloomed around our path, will so guide us onward to a perfect restoration of fraternal affection, that we of this day may be able to transit our great inheritance, of State Governments in all their rights, of the General Government in its whole constitutional vigor, to our posterity, and they to theirs through countless generations?

"ANDREW JOHNSON.

"WASHINGTON, December 4, 1865."

CHAPTER XIX.

CONCLUSION.

PRESIDENT JOHNSON, providentially called to the chief executive chair at an extraordinary crisis, when the country was first emerging from the blood and smoke of a terrible civil war, and when the world was horror-stricken by the news of Lincoln's assassination—President Johnson assumed his onerous duties at a moment's notice, and has since been discharging them with an energy, tact, and discretion that cannot be too highly extolled. Without a parallel in the history of any other people, in its spirit of fraternal magnanimity, stands President Johnson's wise and beneficent policy of reconciliation and reunion. Thus it is that he is accepted by the Southern people, not as a conquering despot, but as a welcome benefactor; and hence their progress in the great task enjoined upon them of rebuilding their State institutions upon the enduring corner-stones of the sovereignty of the Union and universal liberty.

Never did weighter burden press upon a human being than has rested upon the President every moment since he assumed the duties of his exalted station. His doctrine, that the secession of a State could not carry it out of the Union, and that as soon as it grounded its arms it resumed its former status in the federal group, has been of infinite service to him in his well-directed efforts for a speedy restoration. This most desirable object is in a way of rapid accomplishment under his well-planned auspices. His first annual message at the opening of the thirty-ninth Congress, which we have given above, by its calm statement of the situation, and the manifest knowledge of its author how best to meet the political crisis, is so admirably adapted as a safe and rational guide for both legislative and popular action, as to secure for its statements, its reasonings, and its suggestions a strong and universal approbation from the masses of the people. The sympathy of the masses is the firm tower upon which the President leans for support in his future, as he has always done in his past. It has never failed nor deserted him in former times, when, to common observers, all seemed dark and dismal around him, and it will not desert him now. If a rabid fanaticism, if a bitter prejudice shall attempt to oppose his wise and noble policy, he will meet their attacks

> "Firm as a rock of the ocean, that braves
> A thousand wild waves on the shore."

The people, whose Union he will have saved and cemented by bonds that never can be broken, will rally around their honest and dauntless benefactor in the might of an irresistible host. From New England to Texas, from the Old Dominion to the Pacific shore, the name of Andrew Johnson will be dear to the hearts of the people as a household word, and their confiding gratitude will retain him as a worthy occupant of the chair first graced by the Father of his Country.

www.ingramcontent.com/pod-product-compliance
Lightning Source LLC
LaVergne TN
LVHW020228110826
845151LV00003B/855

* 9 7 8 1 4 2 5 5 3 1 7 1 3 *